Prayer's Apprentice

A Year with the Great Spiritual Mentors

TIMOTHY JONES

WORD PUBLISHING
NASHVILLE
A Thomas Nelson Company

Published by Word Publishing, a division of Thomas Nelson Company, P. O. Box 141000, Nashville, Tennessee, 37214.

We have made every effort to trace and contact copyright holders for prayers included in this book. We regret any inadvertent omissions in request for permissions, and we will make appropriate additions and corrections in future editions.

Unless otherwise indicated, Scripture quotations used in this book are from the Holy Bible, New International Version (NIV). Copyright Ó1973, 1978, 1984, International Bible Society. Used by permission of Zondervan Bible Publishers.

Other Scripture references are from:

The New Revised Standard Version of the Bible (NRSV), © 1989 by the Division of Christian Education of the National Council of Churches of Christ in the USA.

The Revised English Bible (REB). Copyright © 1989 Oxford University Press and Cambridge University Press. Used by permission.

See also "Acknowledgments and Permissions" on pages 248-249 which represents a continuation of this copyright page.

Library of Congress Cataloging-in-Publication Data

Jones, Timothy K., 1955–
    Prayers apprentice : a year with the great spiritual mentors / Timothy Jones.
        p. cm.
    ISBN 0-8499-1657-7
        1. Jones, Timothy K., 1955—Diaries. 2. Episcopal Church—Clergy—Diary.
    3. Prayer—Christianity. 4. Spiritual journals. I. Title.

BX5995.J72 A3 2001
242'.2—dc21

00-050329
CIP

Printed in the United States of America
0 1 2 3 4 BVG 9 8 7 6 5 4 3 2 1

To Kevin Miller,
friend and mentor.

Contents

∽∾

MY YEAR OF PRAYERS

Acknowledgments

I thank those who have encouraged me in both the craft of writing and the adventure of prayer: Kevin Miller and Christopher de Vinck. I appreciate the prayers of a number of people who prayed for me while I wrote, especially Gwyn and Mary Lee Bowen and my wife, Jill.

Thanks to those who read portions of the manuscript in process and offered helpful suggestions, especially Kevin Miller and William Griffin, and thanks to Jeanie Hunter, who assisted with typing. I appreciated the skillful and enthusiastic editing of Traci Mullins, president of Eclipse Editorial Services.

Finally, I am grateful to my agent, Bruce Barbour, and the team at Word Publishing, including (but not limited to!) Mark Sweeney, David Moberg, Ami McConnell, Diane Crawford, Diane Wickwire, and Amy Miles.

Mining Spiritual Riches

A couple of years ago, sitting at my desk working on a project (the nature of which I've forgotten), I had a sudden inspiration: What might happen if for an entire year I infused my regular practice of prayer with the recorded prayers of the wisest spiritual teachers? What could I learn? How might my own spiritual life take on new depth and meaning?

That was the beginning of my year of apprenticing myself to a wide range of men and women who, despite centuries and sometimes continents of distance, had much to teach me.

There was a time I would have questioned the value of such an excursion into the prayer lives of others. Doesn't praying what others have formulated lead to a second-hand spirituality? A stiff formality? After all, most of us—including myself—cherish spontaneity in almost everything, no less in our praying. When talking to someone I'm close to, the idea of a script or TelePrompTer seems foreign indeed.

And yet I've learned in recent years that I don't always want to have to "wing it" in the presence of God. Spontaneity is over-rated. "The primary use of prayer," writes author and pastor Eugene Peterson, "is not for expressing ourselves, but in becoming ourselves, and we cannot do that alone."[1] We need mentors and companions. We need instruction. We need patterns to emulate when ours grow tired or slip out of sync.

During this past year of apprenticeship to many wise spiritual forerunners, I have found that others' prayers can help in articulating the yearnings of my heart when my words don't come easily. They help me overcome my occasional dry spells or mumbling impediments.

"For periods of dryness," writes Orthodox priest Anthony Bloom, "we also need some prayers in reserve, which have meant a lot to us at other times. . . . [Praying them,] we should listen intelligently and respond with all that is still alive in us to the familiar words, to words spoken in deserts, by heroes in prayer and the life in God."[2]

And just as black squiggles on a score of music can, when played by a musician, leap to life and create a world of sound and rhythm and emotion, so too can printed prayers come alive. Because the great prayers of the Judeo-Christian tradition span centuries and form a cross section of varied cultures and experiences, I sensed that they could help keep my spirituality from becoming stunted, ingrown. I wanted to draw from the prayers and writings of psalmists and prophets, laborers and scholars, monks and saints, poets and preachers. I wanted such prayers to open my soul to a vast world of spiritual riches.

∽

So began my year with the great spiritual mentors. I told a friend of my project early on. "You're embarking on a considerable pilgrimage," he said. "You never know where it will lead!"

Because I hoped and believed my months with prayer mentors would lead me to discoveries about the spiritual life, I felt it important to keep a journal. I didn't want to lose to a sometimes fuzzy and fickle memory the movements and struggles that might come. And I knew it would be important not to record disembodied insights, but to track what I was discovering in the scenes of real life—my everyday life, in all of its mingled ordinariness and moments of celebration and sadness. I have included in the chapters that follow, one for each week of the year, many of these personal discoveries.

I knew from the start that I might want to share them with others. I wanted to recount what I found and learned. Novelist, essayist, and preacher Frederick Buechner writes, "It seems to me that no matter who you are, and no matter how eloquent or otherwise, if you tell your story with sufficient candor and concreteness, it will be an interesting story and in some sense a universal story. I do it also in the hope of encouraging others to do the same, at least to look back over their own lives, as I have looked back over mine, for certain themes and patterns and signals that are so easy to miss when you're caught up in the process of living them."[3] So I have told what I have seen and heard, staying close to my daily experiences.

With the benefit of time, as I now work on turning the raw material of my journal entries into a book, I have felt free to fill in considerably around the edges. I have developed what in some cases were just jotted impressions, scribbled almost on the run. I have included material and insights that didn't come until I actually sat down and reviewed my material. But the chapters ahead represent fifty-two weeks of my life, a year of daily efforts to pray more faithfully and deeply. They offer glimpses of my heart and, I believe, the life of God in me.

∽

My method of finding prayers barely qualifies as a method. I have allowed my choices to happen serendipitously. Sometimes I found a prayer after a search, other times by seeming accident. What follows cannot claim to be an exhaustive or even representative cross section of all the possibilities. I admit to subjectivity. I do not follow any grand scheme of ordering, other than paying attention to pivotal points of Easter and Christmas (and their periods of preparation in Lent and Advent). Nevertheless, now that I look over the year of weeks, the diversity strikes me. These prayers range far and wide. God has profoundly guided people in many different times and places, and that reassures me that he will surely continue to guide me . . . and you.

How best to read this book of weeks? I do not intend this as a "devotional" as much as a testimony. It is more memoir than manual. Some may read it as they would most any book, from start to finish. Others may benefit from reading a chapter at a time, letting the prayer for that week (and my discoveries or struggles) spark new insight. And spark, I hope, greater desire to mine the vast richness that God makes ours through prayer.

The Road Ahead

My Lord God, I have no idea where I am going. I do not see the road ahead of me, I cannot know for certain where it will end. Nor do I really know myself, and the fact that I think I am following your will does not mean that I am actually doing so. But I believe that the desire to please you does in fact please you. And I hope I have that desire in all that I am doing. . . . And I know that if I do this you will lead me by the right road, though I may know nothing about it. Therefore I will trust you always though I may seem to be lost and in the shadow of death. I will not fear, for you are ever with me, and you will never leave me to face my perils alone. [4]

—THOMAS MERTON

MANY MORNINGS, AS THE SUN RISES IN A hazy sky, I go jogging. I thud along a route on the streets of the Tennessee town where I live, panting and sweating. I may pass an obese woman walking off extra pounds. Or a man opening his front door to let out his sleek black Lab into the yard. Mostly I pass quiet houses and empty cars in driveways.

But I sometimes grow curious. In my mind I see people behind the walls and drawn drapes. I picture middle-aged men, like myself, rolling out of bed, sniffing the aroma of coffee filling the kitchen, pouring Raisin Bran into a bowl, facing off with a sleepy, surly teenager. As they groggily awake, my neighbors must wonder about the day ahead: Will they accomplish the waiting mound of tasks? Will the office routine hold news of a long-awaited promotion? Will a fragile marriage survive? Will a beloved child be safe today?

And I begin wondering about *my* day. I've learned that a lot can transpire in twenty-four hours.

How could I know one Thursday years ago that by evening I would be breathing thanks to God that my family still walked the face of the planet? While my wife and kids headed to my son's allergist, the accelerator on our Chrysler Voyager had stuck to the floor, sending them careening through heavily trafficked Nashville intersections. They dodged cars through a harrowing maze of near collisions, brakes smoking and tires screeching. My wife, Jill, finally ground the car to a halt in a field, shaken but safe. Then she called me at the office where I worked at the time. As she told me calmly on the phone what had happened, *I* felt shaky, my knees weak, just hearing about it all, just imagining what could have happened.

How many are the days that hold the unexpected! Waking up one winter morning almost two decades ago, I could not have known for sure that by day's end I would have finally marshaled courage to tell Jill that I had feelings for her. A group of us from the seminary had taken a bus from Princeton, New Jersey, into New York to see the city. Jill and I had been "just friends"— laughing and silly, sometimes comparing notes on preaching classes. But once back to Princeton, walking with Jill from the bus station to the school, I told her, "I am feeling attracted to you. I'm not sure I should be encouraging these feelings." Given the awkward silence that followed, I could tell *she* certainly had no idea. "I'm flattered," is all she would say. I would learn she had never dreamed that our friendship would end in romance, much less marriage.

Then, years later, as a Virginia summer morning dawned, I would not have guessed that the day's afternoon mail would include a note from a magazine editor responding to an article I had sent in, almost on a whim. I worked as a minister of a mostly rural church south of Roanoke. "We liked your article," the scrawled note said. "We've scheduled it for our October issue." A message that would eventually veer me in a new direction in my career and calling. I might have had occasional glimmers or daydreams, but I could not have predicted the future.

Such are the uncertainties and surprises of many days.

∽

And then there's this morning. Who can imagine, really, what will happen in a day? When I realize this, it's not hard to pray Thomas Merton's prayer, this little acknowledgment of the monk and writer's limited human perspective. So today I pray the line, *I have no idea where I'm going.*

But then I think, *Wasn't he overdramatizing?* Surely Merton, a celebrated priest, activist, and spiritual mentor to millions of readers, knew every morning what to expect from the routine of his cloistered abbey life in rural Kentucky. His day, more than mine, was framed by the prayers of the Daily Office, prayers and spiritual readings ordered in patterns dating back centuries. He worked season after season under the direction of an abbot, sometimes in the monastery's fields, more often at a typewriter in a corner of the massive compound. As Merton became famous after the publication of his memoirs, *The Seven Storey Mountain,* in 1948, many people wanted very much to suggest when he should speak or write a book, where he should go to lead a retreat. *No* idea where he was going? Surely Merton could predict at any hour what would come next.

And it seems like an exaggeration for me, too, to pray that I have *no* idea. This morning, after all, I know a great deal: my mind races ahead to a deadline looming—a book due in mere weeks that is far from done. Even while I think about what awaits me at my desk, my mind thinks through the daily routine of getting my seven-year-old Bekah out the door for school, teaching my seventeen-year-old son Micah in his home-school program, helping Jill dream up something for supper. As I round the corners of my regular jogging route my mind ticks off what today *must* hold. And the next, and the next. As I walk up my sidewalk I know I will see the front screen door with its hinge pulled out from the splintered door facing, a repair long overdue.

I know where I'm going. At least where I think I *need* to go.

But Merton reminds me that I see and understand in only the most tentative sense. Our temptation is to strive to peek ahead, by prayer or by divination to take the uncertainty out of what we cannot know. But none of us have Kodacolor snapshots of tomorrow's turns and long straight stretches. I know what I *want*. But underneath my yearnings runs a current that carries me and others along in ways I see only dimly. I plan, yes; but I also bow to a larger movement of grace and power working in the world. I try my best, but ultimately I must leave results in God's roomy, strong, ordering hands. I cannot come to this day—come to God—bragging about what I'm going to accomplish. Life is too contingent.

My apprenticing myself to the great pray-ers of history, as I begin to do this week, underlines my constant need to "unknow."

Through the year ahead I trust that I will become a deeper, or at least different, person. I hope the prayers I will rummage around in and live and breathe will open me to wider thinking and clearer seeing. But can I say with precision and certitude where they will take me? Of course not.

I am giving up some control over what I pray. Indeed, the very act of praying, like living, requires a suspension of self-command. "Whenever you pray," wrote Henri Nouwen, "you profess that you are not God and that you wouldn't want to be, that you haven't reached your goal yet . . . that you must constantly stretch out your hands for the gift which gives new life."[5] I don't grab as much as stretch out an open palm. Praying of any sort reminds me of how little I can orchestrate, for all my striving and well-intentioned striding forward.

攉

So I face those times when I say with Merton, *I may seem to be lost. . . . and the fact that I think I am following your will does not mean that I am actually doing so.* Merton did get lost, at times, or at least drifted from some of his earlier fervor.

I got literally lost once, out hiking in woods near my house with my daughter. We had a few moments of panic, scant snowflakes dusting our hair and biting our cheeks, before we once again scouted out the path that led home. Our confusion about where we were did not last for longer than fifteen or twenty minutes, but it was bad enough. We kept walking in the direction we thought would lead back to our road, constantly looking at one another with wide eyes and rising fear. And in the bigger ways in which I wander through life and faith, not knowing precisely where I am sometimes feels treacherous. I am not particularly weighed with anxiety today. But there are those other days . . .

Merton helps me here, too. *I will not fear,* Merton said to God, *for you are ever with me, and you will never leave me to face my perils alone.* Even when the anxiety feels powerful and wearying, even then, like I have today, I call to mind that *God is in this. He has not left me alone. He's here.*

☙

Perhaps it is no accident that I have rediscovered Merton's prayer during a week that includes Ash Wednesday. I first found the prayer months ago, printed on a card I bought at the Abbey of Gethsemani in Kentucky, where Merton had lived most of his adult life. This week, when I decided to begin a year of praying with great spiritual mentors, I found the card on a bookshelf where I'd stashed it after the retreat. Now the time seems right to pray it again.

I remember the card in my pocket as I stand in line during the morning Ash Wednesday service I'm attending at the chapel of The Upper Room, part of a church-related agency where I'm working part time. I'm about to kneel and have my forehead imposed with ashes made in the sign of the cross, two quick daubing strokes of charred powder. The minister, Ken Swanson, will tell me, "Remember that you are dust, and to dust you shall return."

Ash Wednesday, Ken has reminded us in his sermon, ushers in Lent, a forty-day period of denial and preparation. The ashes signify and remind me palpably of Good Friday's Cross, the crucifixion of Jesus to come. They hint darkly of the need to wait with longing for Easter's Resurrection. I am made of the dust of creation, they say, and my body will return to that dust as my remains lie moldering.

"Almighty God," Ken prayed during the chapel service, "grant that these ashes may be to us a sign of our mortality and penitence." I am sobered. I pray in utter dependence.

And therein is my freedom. No longer must I feel compelled to compute the outcome of this day, this week, this lifetime. I can open my life and heart and soul to a great, unimaginably wonderful God, trusting that he will lead. *And I know that if I do this,* prayed Merton, who would suffer an accidental death at the age of fifty-three, *you will lead me by the right road though I may know nothing about it.*

I don't live this prayer well, not this week. But every now and then, more by grace than any expertise, I manage it for a moment, maybe for an hour over lunch, perhaps during a morning run.

∽

In other ways I don't see where God is taking me, not really. This week finds me talking to the minister at my church about pursuing ordination in the Episcopal Church, the denomination I joined ten years ago. I'm feeling a divine nudging to ministerial work again. In one sense this is not strange territory; I've been a pastor before. In fact, the mailbox where I got the letter accepting my first article for publication stood on the other side of the road that ran between our house and the church I served. I was ordained in the Church of the Brethren more than twenty years ago, and I pastored that rural congregation with all I had, even as I slowly, strangely felt myself drawn to writing as my vocation. But this time, I think, my ordination would look different: a parish, perhaps, but also a larger "congregation" of those to whom I would continue to write and visit and teach. I don't fit neatly into the standard mold for Episcopal clergy. It's hard to predict where my path will lead, what it might look like, even if I were to be accepted into the intensive ordination process.

And so, again, I have to say I *think* this will happen or I *hope* that will transpire. But I'm reduced to trusting, to following God's lead with few certainties. All I can say is that I believe the road I run along always leads back to home, even when the sun glows dull behind the haze.

Merton knew that. God has the future in mind, even when I can't see it. God will bring me to it and through it.

Tender Reassurance

Two things have I heard: that you, O God, are strong, and that you, O Lord, are loving.

—DAVID, THE PSALMIST

 TODAY I NEEDED THIS PRAYER RECORDED IN Psalm 62. I clutched its promises.

I had shown parts of my book manuscript, the one I'm struggling to finish, to a writer friend for feedback. To call his critique of my work thorough would understate.

"Well," Bill said, after reading a few chapters, "it's pretty repetitious. I felt you were padding the book to make it longer." My personal accounts, the narrative threads, were sketchy, he said, my abstractions too long.

I think I listened graciously (what else could I do?—I had asked for his opinion), but I began to wilt inside. "Hmm," I said, my mind racing to compute the hours of revision his comments could require.

There was a moment of awkward silence between us.

"I've learned that your saying 'hmm' is kind of a verbal tic," Bill finally said.

"I'm trying to process what you're saying," I said. "I'm trying to be open and figure out what it means."

I walked back to my office quietly devastated.

It wasn't just the critique that bothered me. I've given enough suggestions as an editor to know that the best writing often grows out of honest, expert reactions. And, as a writer, I've seen my work analyzed and picked apart and sewn back together. Most writers value another's objectivity. No, it wasn't Bill's criticism that left me reeling. It was my schedule. I was two weeks away from my deadline. And some of the chapters still needed major work. Now I would have to revisit what I thought was already done. It all seemed impossible.

Later in the day, over turkey sandwiches at a local lunch spot, I asked Bill for more comments. I was fishing, I suppose, for reassurance. I got none. Instead, we veered into a conversation about my reading habits. When Bill mentioned authors I had passing or no acquaintance with, he seemed to imply that my reading, something I pride myself on, was anemic.

Sometimes when I feel hard hit with a criticism, I guard my anger or hold my hurt close. Back at my office I tried to carry on with my work, but I had difficulty focusing on my tasks. Outwardly I looked fine, but inside I was very anxious about my book.

Then I discovered the half-sheet of paper in my pocket with this verse from the Psalms on it. I had typed it on a small slip of paper weeks before; that morning, getting ready for work, I had found it in a drawer. Thinking of my new-found discipline of praying and living with others' prayers, I had stuffed David's words in my shirt pocket before I rushed out the door.

And then, as I sat quietly nursing my bruises and fears at my desk, when I needed the psalmist's message most, there it was: *You, O God are strong, . . . you, O Lord, are loving.* I prayed it as a man desperate for reassurance, saying what I hoped to be true as much as what I knew to be true. *This is what I need,* I told myself—*to know that my feckless strength, my little self with its insecurities and weakness, is not the only thing at work, this day, this week.*

So today I tell God he is strong, not because I do him a favor by telling him what he already knows, but because saying it works it into my consciousness. Praying it weaves its assurance into my struggle. I decide to say it, not as a fleeting feeling, but as a truth burnished with centuries of pilgrim prayer and worship: God comes with strength. God can do something! I will not be left feebly floundering.

And in the presence of God, in my crying out for strength, I do more than remember that God has power to turn my mountain of work into a molehill. I catch wind of something even more reassuring: God may be able to act, yes; but even better, God is sure to care. God embodies what the King James Version of the Bible calls loving kindness. *Chesed,* the transliteration of the original Hebrew, carries more weight than our sometimes flimsy words for love. Even the way *chesed* sounds means something. Its initial consonant is like the English "h," but with a delicate guttural definition. Its vocal tone and friction suggests more than soupy love. This is loyal love; it promises to act in a certain way—*for good, for now, forever.* It is compassion pointed in a long direction. It has the staying power, in other words, to help me in this morning's little crisis of self-doubt.

⑨◌

It's later in the week. My manuscript is shaping up. I've been able to reread parts of it with my colleague's comments rolling around in the back of my mind, and I've already made some cuts and polishes that will help. The panic has mostly passed. Things are looking up.

But it's not so much my seeing things I can "fix" that has my equilibrium restored. It's my literally looking *up*. The difference is in praying this psalm.

I thought this morning while exercising, my mind suddenly clear: *This is the nub of faith, isn't it: Is God able to help? And if so, does God* want *to help?* Maybe this is what we ultimately all need to know: Does the God who permeates the universe with majesty also come in tenderness? Will the God Who Is, the One beyond comprehension and measure exercise his power on behalf of his frail creatures?

Last week's prayer of Merton's had me pondering the unknowables—the things I cannot grasp. This week, to my emotional salvation, I find a rock-hard promise to lay hold of.

What of the manuscript that I must complete under the gun? I cannot remove all uncertainty and stress from these coming days. But there will be reminders of unseen help. Surely there will be reminders. And so I will keep praying with hope.

Honest to God

The prayer preceding all prayers is *"May it be the real I who speaks. May it be the real Thou that I speak to."*[6]
—C. S. LEWIS

 DID I GO TOO FAR? THAT IS THE QUESTION nagging at me today.

Last night I drove hurriedly a half-hour to the Nashville airport post office, taking advantage of its late-night mail pickup. I had been up since dawn, indeed had been working through the weekend and evenings, pushing hard to finish my book. The middle-aged postal clerk was jovial, though, glad for his nine o'clock quitting time just minutes away. I made it. Barely. Now the manuscript is on its way to the publisher.

I am relieved to be done, but also a little anxious. I entertain not just the nagging anxieties you would expect in an author finishing a book: *Was my prose clear? Will I get through to the reader?* No, this time I wrestled with other fears that hit closer to the bone: *Did I get too personal? Will I embarrass myself?*

Friends who had read early drafts had encouraged me to speak honestly, revealingly. So I did. I spoke of conflicts with loved ones, of spiritual doubts I wrestle with. I stayed close to my daily experiences, opening my heart. But in my vulnerable moments, I inwardly cringe at the unflattering particulars. I feel exposed when I think of thousands of people peering into the details of my daily life.

It is not just writing for publication that provokes anxieties, of course. In daily conversation, who of us doesn't wonder how much we dare to reveal of our joys and pains? When someone asks us, "How are you?" most of us invariably say, "Fine!" even if we're not. We feel pressure to be perky, "together." Sometimes I feel compelled to hide all hurt, afraid that revealing it only exposes my weakness.

On the other hand, sometimes our culture holds out as the ideal people who dump out, like they would an overloaded gunny sack, all they feel and fear and hope for. Our culture of "personal vulnerability" encourages us to do so with no sensitivity to the awkwardness we may create. We feel pressure to prove how "authentic" we can be. Such a climate makes me grow weary of people taking my emotional temperature. I don't always want to have to reach in and grasp my beating, hurting heart and place it on the table for public examination. So I grow used to guarding my deepest self, its fears and dreams and hopes.

As I pick up the book containing Lewis's simple words and pray them, I find worrying about all this becomes a moot point. At least when I talk to God.

I can try to make myself look good in prayer, of course, by primping and impressing. I can hold close my dark thoughts, suppress my shame, or play-act my piety. I can hide, I suppose, if through no other means than by simply not showing up for prayer. But why bother? I have enough sense to know that God, who hears all and sees all, won't be fooled. Nor will he be evaded.

On Sundays in church I come to God saying the Episcopal liturgy, "to you all hearts are open, all desires known, and from you no secrets are hid." I have read in the New Testament that "Nothing in all creation is hidden from God's sight. Everything is uncovered and laid bare before the eyes of him to whom we must give account" (Hebrews 4:13). I know I cannot hide or evade for long.

What of the pressure to unload all in some cathartic heart-dump? Somehow that seems beside the point as well, at least in the presence of a God for whom anything I say can never be a surprise.

In this sense, then, I do not hesitate much in coming to God with my "real I" when I speak to him. And in this sense perhaps I am different from C. S. Lewis, the atheist who went through early adulthood with no room for belief in God. Lewis the scholar who hid behind his books and papers and intellectualisms. Lewis who wanted to *run*.

> You must picture me alone in that room in Magdalen [a college at Oxford University], night after night, feeling, whenever my mind lifted even for a second from my work, the steady, unrelenting approach of Him whom I so earnestly desired not to meet. That which I greatly feared had at last come upon me. In the Trinity Term of 1929 I gave in, and admitted that God was God, and knelt and prayed: perhaps, that night, the most dejected and reluctant convert in all England. I did not then see what is now the most shining and obvious thing; the Divine humility which will accept a convert even on such terms. The Prodigal Son at least walked home on his own feet. But who can duly adore that Love which will open the high gates to a prodigal who is brought in kicking, struggling, resentful, and darting his eyes in every direction for a chance of escape? [7]

My resistance is far from that dramatic; my conversion was not nearly so climactic. Yet in another sense I am much like Lewis. The word *real* can mean "absolute, complete, utter." This is part of what we mean when we say of someone who doesn't hide a part of himself or deal in relational evasions, "Bob is *real*." We sense that we are dealing with the whole person, not a showy part carefully meted out or managed.

Here is how I need to pray for a real "I": *Help me, God, to bring you my whole self.* I hardly love God with my whole heart and soul, mind, and strength, as Jesus commanded. I like to retain jurisdiction over at least a quadrant of self. I hold on tight to its whims and wants. I dole out what I think I can give to God in teaspoons, not in overflowing measures.

But as a result I end up fragmented. Guarded. My faith becomes half-hearted.

So now I pray, *Let it be the whole, complete I. Not, O God, the I too eager to invite into the living room of my soul the distractions I think will help me avoid encountering you alone. Not the petty I, with all my fretting and incessant refusal to sit still in your presence. Not the fickle I, my affections for you hot one moment, blasé the next. I don't want to hold back anything. I want to come I to Eye. I want to be the real thing.*

Lewis eventually wanted, when he came to pray, to settle for nothing less than a genuine heart. Lewis knew that in prayer he could become more and more true to himself, less and less the impostor or faker or dodger. That is what I want. What I pray for, here and now.

And, I realize, during this season of Lent, this time of repentance and examination, real prayer takes place when I stop acting like everything is okay even if it's not. Toyohiko Kagawa, the Christian who moved many at the midpoint of the twentieth century with his ministry among Japan's desperately poor, wrote about Jesus' praying in the Garden of Gethsemane, prayer made agonizingly frank by the Cross he knew was to come. Wrote Kagawa, "Had [Jesus] only said, 'Thy will be done,' it would not have been a prayer. It is the words, 'Let this cup pass away from me' which make it a true prayer."[8]

It is those words that made Jesus' prayer truly human, his cry that of One who was not only fully God, but also fully one of us. And for me, for all of us, Lewis discovered, it is honest prayer that will keep us coming back.

∽

Now, near the end of the week, I wonder, *How do I sustain this new desire to be real, to be honest to God? How do I come fully, not half-heartedly?*

Much of the answer has to do with trust.

Kenneth Wilson tells of growing up in Pittsburgh, taking this lesson to heart: "That house in which we lived on the side of one of Pittsburgh's hills was three stories high in the front and four in the back. The bottom layer was the cellar and the top was what we called the third floor, really a finished attic, the ceiling of which was cut into shadowed geometric shapes by dormer windows. Up there were two bedrooms, a hallway, and a mysterious storage room for trunks that always smelled of mothballs and history. Our family slept there, because the second floor was usually rented out for a 'tenant' to help pay the rent."

Kenneth remembers that, being the youngest, he had to go to bed first, braving that floor of dark bedrooms. It felt like a long way up the steps, especially because they did not have electricity above the second floor, and a gas light had to be turned on, then turned off once the boy was settled.

That bed in that room on the third floor seemed to be at the end of the earth, remote from human habitation, close to unexplained noises and dark secrets. At my urging, my father would try to stop the windows from rattling, wedging wooden match sticks into the cracks. But they always rattled in spite of his efforts. Sometimes he would read me a story, but inevitably the time would come when he would turn out the light and shut the door and I would hear his steps on the stairs, growing fainter and fainter. Then all would be quiet, except for the rattling windows and my cowering imagination.

Once, I remember, my father said, "Would you rather I leave the light on and go downstairs, or turn the light out and stay with you for awhile?" You can guess [what I chose: his] presence with darkness, over absence with light."[9]

The assurance that Someone is there—more real than our fears—is that not what we want most?

Now, thinking about the God I approach, with what I hope is *more* of myself than before, I find it easier to come without fear. Knowing how I am already known and met and accompanied helps me pray without my guard up. I can do so because of an assurance of Someone *there*, Presence even in darkness.

An Insatiable Yearning

You called and cried out loud and shattered my deafness. You were radiant and resplendent, you put to flight my blindness. You were fragrant, and I drew in my breath and now pant after you. I tasted you, and I feel but hunger and thirst for you. You touched me, and I am set on fire to attain the peace which is yours. [10]

—AUGUSTINE

I MAY AS WELL ADMIT IT: I FEEL IN OVER MY head with this prayer. I feel drawn to it, of course, but I cannot shake the sense that it comes from someone whose inner self is larger than mine.

"The house of my soul," Augustine had prayed elsewhere to great effect, "is too small for you to come to it. May it be enlarged by you." God must have at least begun to answer. And in this prayer Augustine pulls in every sense possible to make his petition. Here is someone with an insatiable yearning for God. He wanted no part of himself untouched, unnourished, unmet.

As I sit with his words this morning in my living room, the house quiet and dark before others are up, I realize that ironies abound: The one-time profligate and wanderer after falsehood found a profound, life-gripping faith. But he knew he could never be through with his seeking. For all he grasped about his faith, this fourth-century African bishop, this author of a masterpiece of literature known as the *Confessions*, still knew that a faithful heart must be willing to *unlearn*. He would have to let go day by day, and open wider. His restiveness would become a restlessness for God.

Today, Augustine hits me over the head with a reminder to nourish that longing within myself. Sometimes I don't get quiet enough to notice it. I go blithely along. Like this morning, distracted, struggling to sit still long enough to pray. Even before that, lying in bed but eager to get going, I tell myself, *I have so much to do at the office.* Since we are home schooling my son Micah, I know I will sit down with him sometime today to check on his progress. The things clamoring to get done crowd in hard.

But I also want something else in my better moments. Some*one* else. I don't want life's fine print to crowd out this Loving God. Remembering that helps me to resist bending under the weight of urgent doings and comings and goings. "The simple desire for God is already the beginning of faith," I remember Brother Roger of Taize once said. Just my wanting counts for something.

So I pray, as I begin this week, *God, increase my desire. Let me seek you through this prayer, and in seeking to find, be found. However small the room of my soul, perhaps you will come and grow in me.* Augustine's words evoking all my senses may create a larger space for that to happen.

࿇

You called and cried out loud and shattered my deafness. You do not speak in code or always whisper. You call. You cry aloud.

I find myself awed at such initiative. Is this not getting to the root of what I most long for? Who does not want to hear his or her name called out? I yearn to be noticed. But this hearing of

God is not something I will make happen. At least not on my own. I can be ready, but it takes more waiting than forcing. I begin not by merely trying harder, but by opening my life to what God wants to do.

The very structure of the prayer shows this. This coming does not start with "I," with something *I* must *do* as though all hinged on me. No, it begins with God. *God* called. God reaches out.

On a lark I decide to count pronouns. In Augustine's prayer the word *you,* God as the object of address, appears eight times, the word *I* only four. *You* cried aloud. *You* touched me. The movement comes from above. My part has more to do with responding than setting things in motion.

So I try to listen in case God has something to say. Some word of assurance for my anxieties about all I have to get done. Some word of forgiveness for my sadness over my self-centeredness. Some cleansing of my shame.

But I have trouble hearing. Henri Nouwen writes, "We have often become . . . unable to know when God calls us and unable to understand in which direction he calls us." [11] Nouwen goes on to say that our lives have thereby become absurd, for in the word *absurd* we find the Latin word *surdus,* which means "deaf." In contrast, Nouwen explains, the word *obedient* comes from the Latin *audire,* which means "listening." Listening turns an absurd life into an obedient one, he says. It makes for an interior roominess, a capacity for sound to be heard.

But even that is not enough. It takes God shattering my deafness, my defensiveness. It requires a God willing to overcome my faulty hearing.

I think of my hard-of-hearing, late father-in-law, a locomotive engineer, his ears scarred and deadened from years of standing behind old steam engines in a closed cab. When I knew him, he had a hearing aid that, while it helped him pick up sounds, magnified *all* sound. The volume overwhelmed his auditory nerves. In a crowded room he got jumpy. The hearing aid could not help him discriminate certain sounds. In a hall full of people he had trouble hearing the *one* word amid the many. Conversation with more than one or two was difficult.

How I need help to discern and sort in that deeper level of the heart. Fortunately, Augustine reminds me, God can help me to listen. And God is not mute, like those who say he made the world and stepped back, never to intervene or interfere. *God save me from my deafness.*

∾

Another day. *You were radiant and resplendent, you put to flight my blindness.* Out running this morning, I felt again how beyond me this prayer is. My daily life appears simple and unspectacular.

But *God?* God is another story.

Radiant in splendor, this prayer reminds me. God is the most interesting thing there is to see or notice. He is one who catches our wandering eyes and lights up our dim viewpoint.

While I ran I spent some time thinking about this God who Augustine found wonderful beyond imagining. All around me I noticed rolling clouds, saw the shifting sunlight dancing on the hills beyond the valley beneath the road by my house. Little smoke signals from a hidden fire, yet they suggest unaccountably marvelous wonders. My little life didn't seem so small, not when I realized how God infuses it with glimmers of his kindness and glory.

I also found myself beginning to pray big prayers about my interest in ordination and in starting a ministry focused on nourishing prayer. By the stream at the end of one of the roads where I run, I took a tuft of moss and threw it into the rushing brook. I took a dead oak leaf and did the same thing. Both got halted in their downstream progress, caught in the watery plants or rocks in the stream bed. Then I took a small green leaf of a watercress-like plant, and it sailed on down the rushing water, quickly out of sight. I thought, *May God carry me along like that, without obstacles put up by me.* May I have the clear vision to let God be God.

෬

You were fragrant and I drew in my breath and now pant after you. It is later still in the week. Last night Jill was going through a gardening magazine. She came across an article on lilacs, a flower desperately important to someone who grew up in North Dakota, where, with its long winters and short growing seasons, lilacs are one of the few flowering plants that thrive. Several varieties of the lush, lavender blooms spread across the pages. But it was the fragrance, even the bare recollection of it, that brought back Jill's memories most powerfully. "I can close my eyes and draw in my breath and still smell them," she said. She found herself transported to those bright spring days.

How potent our sense of smell, how important in reading our environment, in experiencing the beauty of creation. How tied in with our need for air and the oxygen we gasp after when winded. We long for fresh air when cooped up in a dank and foul-smelling cellar. *All the more do we need the life-giving sweet fragrance of your presence.* And so I pray, *Help me inhale the sweetness of your goodness, permeating and pervading the scenes of my life, reminding me of what I might forget.*

Today, another day, another sense to pray with, and I pick up the phrase, *I tasted you, and I feel but hunger and thirst for you.* I kept saying the words this morning during my prayer time. I did not feel a great influx of energy and power, only a hunger, only a longing for God. Not in an intense way, as someone does who is famished, but in a steady way, as someone who feels he cannot get by without regular meals.

I began thinking of how I want to give God the highest place in my life. But how? When gratitude comes naturally to my lips and heart, I do so more easily, most of the time. But *always?* In every circumstance?

In the past couple of days, since we've added a puppy to our household, with all the demands it makes—needing to be taken out to relieve himself, needing to held, needing to be kept away from gnawing on furniture—it has been harder to pray. Jill has been feeling "spiritually tired." So that adds to my feelings of quiet need, aching hunger. But I also know inconvenience helps me pray, when I let it. And I realize again how that is a key to "tasting" the Lord.

∞

You touched me, and I am set on fire to attain the peace which is yours. God, I believe, generally brushes up against us lightly. God intersects our lives through events that remind us of his care, through friends who mediate his presence, through a sense of quiet nearness that may steal upon us as we sit on our porch or enter the hush of an old church. I feel great longing for him, sometimes, for the One who subtly draws near. And the barest touch keeps alive and awake the longing.

I began this prayer saying how in over my head I felt. Now I see how little this prayer hinges on me, how much on God. This week the movement from my side comes simply—through listening, watching, hungering, waiting for a reassuring touch.

The senses of my soul will cry out—and in my yearning I will be met by a radiant, resplendent, fragrant God.

The God of Mixed Blessings

O Eternal and most gracious God, the God of security, and the enemy of security, too, who wouldst have us always sure of thy love, and yet wouldst have us always doing something for it. Let me always so apprehend thee as present with me, and yet so follow after thee as though I had not apprehended thee. [12]

—JOHN DONNE

AS I FLIPPED THROUGH JOHN DONNE'S writings, a book that has sat on my shelves unopened for years, this prayer stood my soul at attention. I found myself unsettled by and yet drawn to it.

I talked about it with Jill. For while she favors discipline in the Christian life, my wife reacted with a frown when I read it to her, as we sat in the car in between running errands, eventually stopping for coffee at a bookstore cafe. She frowned especially at the part about "always doing something" for God's love. As though we can never rest in knowing God holds us. As though we must always strive. That picture of our life with God seemed to her so austere. I had a similar reaction at first.

But that's not how I take it when I read the prayer carefully. When I *pray* it. What I believe Donne was after was captured in what a friend said recently, a friend having trouble mustering energy for prayer. Even so, she said, she refused to give up. "I am determined to move from my level, middle-of-the-road Christianity," she said, "where I can rest on what I comfortably believe about God, to actually *knowing* God." She knew she needed to count on God's fathomless love, yet not get complacent in her pursuit of him.

I learned from last week's prayer how little good it does to try to barge in as though only I can make things happen. And yet I cannot just slouch around God, either. Somehow each movement must find its appropriate place. Today I need to expend effort to do what I can, but also leave room for great grace. It is a tension. How much comes as gift? And then how much depends on my effort? I wrestle with such questions this very week, as it turns out, struggling to be faithful in prayer when the house of my soul seems disquieted, distracted. Trying to be more sensitive to my kids when irritability rises from deep within.

I think that must be something of the spirit behind Donne's prayer. Donne, so sophisticated that his Renaissance poetry would stir readers for centuries to come, had come finally to realize that everything significant in his life hinged on God. And yet he could not stay passive, either.

I come to discover, as I read more about Donne, how he sensed the tension keenly, striving for words that he knew could only faintly depict the struggle: The God who washes away our cowering guilt, yet the God who wants us anxious for the kingdom of God. *The God of security, and the enemy of security, too.* God moves to accomplish his will, yet wants me to participate in the outcome of what he gets going.

So I look for God, discern what the Divine Hand is already shaping, in both the quiet times and tumultuous moments. I accept God's goodness and then wake up every morning and do my work. I open my hands in prayer knowing how much God's blessing will matter, but I also make my calls and write my paragraphs with what I hope is nothing less than my best. That is the tension of faithfulness. Or perhaps, better said, the rhythm.

∾

Donne's life straddled the sixteenth and seventeenth centuries, a time of great social turmoil. The Black Death (bubonic plague) still flared and raged occasionally. When Donne was just a toddler, across the channel French Protestants were slaughtered in bloody religious controversy. His own parents were Catholic in a pro-Protestant England. Donne's brother landed in prison for "harboring" a Catholic priest at his college dorm, a cell in which he would eventually die. Donne agonized over the rifts. Was truth held, he wondered, by Catholic or Protestant, the Pope or the Church of England? For a time Donne drifted from much faith at all. He circled back again and again.

I am at mid-life, as Donne likely was when he penned this prayer—perhaps one reason I have been drawn to praying it. As an assistant to a public official, the younger Donne had swelled with ambition. Now, as he prays, he sees clearer. So do I. His aspirations have been tempered. As have mine. Some of my grand plans for my career have met with more modest realities. Yet I somehow always want to shine and excel in ways that seem to elude my simpler talents, or my quieter place in the scheme of things.

Another turn of events nearly ruined Donne. The problem came when he fell in love. Marriage to his beloved, the teenage Ann More, seemed remote. Her father, Sir George More, a favorite of Queen Elizabeth, resolutely blocked the way. Ann's father was hunting for a more suitable groom, someone with more cachet, more prestige and wealth. Sir George cared nothing about the feelings the two might cherish. Even Donne's modest claim to fame, his sensuous poetry, became a mark against him in the eyes of the reputation-conscious Sir George.

Donne was not easily stopped in romance, however, as later he would not be thwarted in his response to a stormy courtship with a Divine Other, *the God of security, and yet the enemy of security, too.* When Donne learned that Ann was coming to London for a visit in October 1601, the two met secretly. They plotted a clandestine marriage. It would force her father's hand, Donne reasoned. And keep them together.

Once wed, Ann returned home with her father so as to keep the secret intact. When Donne finally told her father what they had done after weeks of whipping up his courage, all fury broke loose. I have a feeling for what he experienced, having told my own parents of my plans to marry Jill, only to have them disapprove. There would be no parental blessing for my marriage until years after the fact. Donne met again *the God of security and yet the enemy of security, too.*

Because Donne had married a minor without parental consent, flagrantly ignoring canon law, Sir George had no trouble getting Donne imprisoned. Donne's employer fired him. Career prospects vaporized.

As things heated up in Donne's personal life, the unexpected turns would fuel his reaching out for a God of mixed blessings, a God who could suckle and a God who could goad. In the strange workings of God's grace, Donne's new insecurity (indeed, years to come of poverty) worked a profound change in Donne. While he managed to gain freedom from his jail cell, and while the courts rebuffed Sir George's efforts at annulling his daughter's marriage, and while Donne soon managed to reconcile with his father-in-law, Donne would never act the same. Essays and poems from this time take on a more spiritual quality, a deeper, more sober tone.

Time was kind to the marriage relationship, some consolation for all it cost Donne. He and Ann had several children.

But even this earthly contentment would soon be denied Donne. Ann died in the wake of a miscarriage. Donne was heartbroken, *undone,* as one coy observer put it in a play on words. It was here and now, however, that Donne's faith deepened. *Let me always so apprehend thee as present with me,* he prayed, reaching out amidst the pain of loss.

I asked a friend who had studied Donne how Donne meant that word *apprehend,* now used mainly to refer to nabbing someone: "Police *apprehended* two men believed to have robbed a bank." But there is another, more likely meaning, I had thought, and my friend confirmed: Donne used the word to mean *comprehend.* As in: *Help me to grasp you in my understanding.* As in: *Help me to know you.*

Such were the cries of a desperate man, living on the edge of a culture that both admired him and could turn on him, wink at his indiscretions or imprison him. Donne was reduced to essentials. *And yet [let me] so follow after thee as though I had not apprehended thee.* To whom else could he turn? To whom else can any of us turn when the way ahead seems blocked?

೧৩

Jill just wrote to a dear friend of ours and showed me the correspondence, letting me in on how better to pray for Eleanor's tough times. I already knew our friend was struggling with anger at God over what she saw as an almost disastrous relocation related to her husband's job. They had—with all four children— been uprooted and sent several states away to a community that felt distant in more ways than one.

Jill had said the appropriately and genuinely supportive things in her letter, of course. But then she asked, "Could it be that God found some cracks in the foundation of how you were approaching life before and wants to build up and repair that foundation?" Jill knew she was taking a risk to write that way to Eleanor. "You feel weak and whiny, you say," Jill continued. "Could that just be because God has removed the old grout exposing the cracks? If so, weak and whiny is the first step toward strong and confident. I know that you are loved and approved of and accepted beyond what you can even ask or imagine. I know that because I love you and approve of you and accept you, and I'm not always a very loving person. How much more the God who is love must love you."

It was not a completely gentle word, but by God's grace it was just what our friend needed, judging by her letter of response, a letter full of insight and gratitude. God was bringing Eleanor to a new and difficult place. It was an austere mercy, but God was not leaving her stranded. In her broken loneliness, the God of insecurity became a God of a more certain security.

So also Donne discovered, in his own way. He found that God was not done with Donne, no matter how he would struggle in his humanness. God had other plans for the crafter of flashy poetry. God ordained paths that would turn out better (if not easier) than a secure position in His Majesty's court.

For finally yet another blow came: King James read Donne's essays and, impressed, wanted Donne to become a priest in the Church of England, serving as a kind of Protestant trophy in religiously contentious times. The king, to force Donne's hand, intervened every time Donne pursued an appointment in public service. He schemed to keep Donne from the option of anything save the priesthood. For several years Donne lived in a kind of vocational dark night of the soul, every avenue to his own desires blocked.

Did Donne dare pray again to One he knew could be *the enemy of security?* Did he somehow sense what was coming in prayer, or know it simply by the doors constantly slamming in his face? How much he stood to lose by responding to God's call, he thought. His poet's acclaim, perhaps. His enjoyment of the literary scene. And yet circumstances kept reminding him that he had nothing to lose, not anything truly vital. And so Donne caved in to the king's persistence, kicking, if not exactly screaming. Donne turned to God, though perhaps some days he wanted to turn *on* God.

And the God of mixed blessings used the king's conniving in a wonderful way: A poet became a preacher. The rhyming lover became a dignified clergyman. Soon it was Donne's sermons and devotional writings, not his romantic poetry, that became the buzz.

His life would not somehow become sheltered from inner and outer conflict, of course. Not in the way some mistakenly envision the spiritual life as devoid of ups and downs and filled only with fuzzy sentiments. In Donne's case the divine Wrestler would have to wrest victory from a resistant fighter. Donne may have consented, but you can imagine how he still struggled some mornings, when, instead of a blank tablet awaiting his lofty verse, he faced a cranky parishioner.

Donne, who had lived hard, ambitiously, passionately, must have wondered what people thought as he mounted his pulpit on Sundays. His story resembled Augustine's, whose writings Donne often quoted. Both wrestled with a past, with claiming their inheritance as children of God.

୭୦

This week as I pray about my own vocation, I wrestle, too. Vocation has been a sometime thorn for me, as it has been for many. I hear two callings: to write and to minister. To pen books and yet to pastor. The callings are not exclusive, as Donne would prove, but in practice the demands of one often compete with the obligations of the other. Whatever one's calling or efforts to hear what God wants, sometimes the working out does not come easily.

I know my struggles all too well, my preference for the easy way, my propensity to let anxiety cloud my vision of God, my petty desires, and self-involved fantasies. How eagerly I volunteer for middle-class comfort and squirm at the prospect of sacrifice. Some days I would cringe to have broadcast on a Jumbotron all my tenacious insecurities and seething ambitions.

But I will remember that God cradles my life. Not that God resembles a celestial errand boy, not that God indulges me lightly. Yet he is not a distant, uninvolved father either. No, this is a God who surrounds and enfolds my every coming and going.

This morning I am more struck by the need simply to be and to do as I can, by the grace of God, what God wants. I write on a Saturday in late March, reclining on our back deck. Warmth surrounds me, a great sky wraps around me—almost cloudless, just wisps here and there, toward the west a gathering bank of clouds. Perhaps it will rain? I don't know. But for now spring seems ready to burst forth, already showing in the buds, dusting the far-off trees on the other side of the valley with lacy, pale greens.

The beauty and awesomeness of what I see hints of One who watches and waits, one who allows the pain of crucifixion but transmutes it into new life: *The enemy of security, and the God of security, too.* This God, I realize for at least this moment, wants for me a truer security than I could ever find in finite happinesses I settle for. Or strive for. Such a God, set against my petty desires and puny goals, is ultimately my friend.

God's Graceful Reordering

Almighty God, you alone can bring into order the unruly wills and affections of sinners: Grant your people grace to love what you command and desire what you promise; that, among the swift and varied changes of the world, our hearts may surely there be fixed where true joys are to be found; through Jesus Christ our Lord, who lives and reigns with you and the Holy Spirit, one God, now and for ever. Amen. [13]

—THE BOOK OF COMMON PRAYER

LAST NIGHT DID NOT EXACTLY LAUNCH ME into the week well-rested: I packed for the festival on faith and writing in Grand Rapids, where I'm leading a panel, gave the puppy a bath, and helped Micah with his Ancient Civilization home school class. On top of all that, my back is acting up. I'm starting this week frazzled.

This morning, though, begins to look different. I ride the air currents on a jet soaring 45,000 feet above the ground—the family set, the dog happy, the most pressing work as done as it can be, a time away stretching before me. I finally feel able to relax enough to catch a breath, to open myself undistractedly to God.

And I do, right on the plane. *You alone,* I say silently, *can bring into order the unruly wills and affections of sinners.*

I think my past few days have been unruly not so much in

flagrant defiance of God's ways, but more through the chaos of a too-filled life. We are too busy, someone one said, because we are lazy, because we find it simpler to be driven by others' claims and compulsions instead of braving the risky work of saying "no." We prefer to feel indispensable even though it makes our schedules barely manageable. In my case, what I fill my life with is not *wrong*—these involvements that all seem so valid and valuable. And I want to do them. But sometimes too many good things, one piled on another and on another, cease to be good.

My prayer this week, though, helps me remember to ask, *Can God help me sort out what stretches before me? Can God capture the attention of my wandering affections, my headstrong will?* I certainly have tried to rein them in myself often enough. But the prayer reminds me of what gives the discipline a shred of hope: God's graceful reordering.

How do I let it happen? I read something by Eugene Peterson, a wise mentor if ever our day has one. He was talking about the need for simplicity. "When others are telling you to do more, I want to tell you to do less. The world does not need more of you; it needs more of God. Your friends do not need more of you; they need more of God. And you don't need more of you; you need more of God."[14]

I keep praying that God would help me see that, and thereby gently re-order me. Rebalance me.

ॐ

But then I snag on the word *sinners. Me?* That bad? Sometimes I snap at my children, yes. A few times I have shouted them down in a rage, leaving their little spirits withered. I turn my face away from the poor. I have steadfastly refused to become regular with the discipline of fasting. My soul often wanders when I sit in the presence of a holy, infinitely awesome God.

So yes, I fall short. Definitely.

But what this prayer is after goes much deeper, I suspect, this prayer lodged in the venerable *Book of Common Prayer,* with roots that go back centuries: The point is not anyone's specific sins, whether they be hidden and respectable or long-listed and gross. No, I am a sinner simply because of my predilection for Tim over God. It is my self-fixation that does me in. Jesus said only the one willing to lose his or her life would find it. How rarely do I "lose" myself in God. I try to cram-pack my life with myself, not others or God. And that gets me in trouble. It means a life "bent" away from God.

Sometimes in the early morning as I lay in bed, unable to go back to sleep, I will use a prayer from the Eastern Orthodox tradition. That helps some. The words remind me of my constant need for grace. It is a prayer I say quietly under my breath, usually just in my mind, called the Jesus Prayer, handed down from centuries of practice and veneration. The shortened form employs just seven words: "Lord Jesus Christ, have mercy on me." The longer version adds a title for Jesus: "Lord Jesus Christ, *Son of the living God . . .*" and adds a word for me: "have mercy on me, *a sinner.*" Whether I use the longer form or the shorter, the prayer reminds me of how I live by mercy, not by my own ingenious goodness. I cannot get by without grace, no matter how hard I try to be virtuous. Such a prayer helps me stay humble and grateful, just as the longer prayer from *The Book of Common Prayer* does.

I don't go around all the time bemoaning my sins. I don't wear a hair shirt or whip my back with spiked cords like a medieval monk. Such ascetic excesses are not my temptations! But I cannot forget my humbling need for mercy. I come to God admitting what I am. It is not all I want to be, but it is what *is,* and therefore what God and I have to work with.

"People divide into two types:" writes Philip Yancey, "not the guilty and the 'righteous,' as many people think, but rather two different types of guilty people. There are guilty people who acknowledge their wrongs, and guilty ones who do not."[15] Sinners who admit, he goes on to say, and sinners who deny. I want not to forget who I am.

And I want to remember that I am a sinner because it keeps before me my constant debt to the Forgiver. To use the word "sinner," archaic as it seems in these postmodern times, eliciting images of hell-fire sermons, jars me just enough to appreciate how mercifully God forgives—how he waits to lead me out of the false promise of a Godless life into the freedom of a forgiven, grace-filled life . . . when I let him.

∞

Inviting God in to do that, I realized this day after my conference ended and the jet plane brought me home, that much of my job is simply to make room. The old tension, just as I felt last week with John Donne's prayer, crops up again. Eugene Peterson reminds me of this interplay of what I do and what God does, of submission and activism, of God's doing and my receiving. Peterson tells of discovering, as a student studying ancient Greek, the verb form, unusual to us, of the "middle voice."

It took him weeks to get it. But this form brought a stab of insight about how it is with our life with God. The middle voice, he explained, is not the active voice, where I describe my doing something or initiating an action that goes somewhere: "I counsel my friend." Nor is it the passive voice, where I receive the action another does or initiates. As in, "I am counseled by my friend." No, the middle voice points to an action *already* begun that *I participate in.* As in, "I take counsel."

And this applies to prayer, says Peterson; there, too, the action comes not as either/or, but both/and: God's grace *and* my penitence. God's gift of mercy and my responding in grateful reception. So I pray my prayer this week in middle voice, as Peterson says prayer should be:

> I do not control the action; that is a pagan concept of prayer, putting the gods to work by my incantations or rituals. I am not controlled by the action; that is a Hindu concept of prayer in which I slump passively into the impersonal and fated will of gods and goddesses. I enter into the action begun by another, my creating and saving Lord, and find myself participating in the results of the action. I neither do it, nor have it done to me; I will to participate in what is willed.[16]

Another day . . . and in the morning, even before the day gets rolling, I find myself sobered by a passage from Jeremiah, that wailing, weeping prophet who spoke to a culture coming unglued from its faithlessness. He railed against a people he loved. He pointed them back to a God both agonized and angry at their fickleness. I read the passage as part of the Daily Office Lectionary, a set of readings from the Old and New Testament for each day in *The Book of Common Prayer,* the worship book for Episcopalians. I don't get to them every day, for all my good intentions. But I try. And this morning's words from the prophet will not let me get comfy in my middle-class securities and easy beliefs.

This word came from the Lord to Jeremiah. Stand at the gate of the Lord's house and there make this proclamation: Hear the word of the Lord, all you of Judah who come in through these gates to worship him. These are the words of the Lord of Hosts the God of Israel: Amend your ways and your deeds, that I may let you live in this place. You keep saying, 'This place is the temple of the Lord, the temple of the Lord, the temple of the Lord!" This slogan of yours is a lie; put not trust in it. If you amend your ways and your deeds, deal fairly with one another, cease to oppress the alien, the fatherless, and the widow, if you shed no innocent blood in this place and do not run after other gods to your own ruin, then I shall let you live in this place. (Jeremiah 7:1–7, REB)

I think the "slogan" was a lie not because it was not true (was it not, after all, the temple that God guided as it was built?) but because it represented the people's presumption. They assumed they could live in disregard for God and his ways. God's mercy would be their fall-back. What nerve!

And so I pray this morning: *I know you as a God of grace, but let me not presume. Help me not to take you for granted.*

⬦

It is Good Friday, the day when so many believers around the world recall Jesus' painful death. "My Father," prayed Jesus in the Garden of Gethsemane on the eve of his crucifixion, "if it is possible, may this cup be taken from me. Yet not as I will, but as you will" (Matthew 26:39).

Help me desire what you promise, this week's prayer says. This is another way, I suspect, for my unruly will and affections to find their place. I learn to want what God wants, what God wills, what God waits to do. This takes some doing. What if what God promises does not jibe with my cherished ambitions? Paul the apostle's words pierce me:

"I have been crucified with Christ and I no longer live, but Christ lives in me. The life I live in the body I live by faith in the son of God, who loved me and gave himself for me" (Galatians 2:20). Paul's was not an easy life, for all its joys. And the cross Jesus faced, I cannot forget, led him into inhuman treatment and untold suffering.

And so I have to ask again, what if God's great and gracious promises come attached with a cost? This is the question that makes me have to pray that I will, after all, *want* what God promises.

But then I read another verse, again from Jeremiah, that helps. "For I know the plans I have for you," says the Lord, speaking through the prophet, "plans to prosper you and not to harm you, plans to give you hope and a future" (Jeremiah 29:11). "I alone know," the verse begins in one translation. *God alone knows.*

So whatever the "swift and varied changes of the world," as my prayer has it, God is working something out. I will try to let go of my frantic need to control for yet another moment, yet another day. Too many good things can come out of a heart yielded to God, I conclude. Here is my hope: resurrection out of crucifixion, dancing out of mourning, a steady groundedness when things shake and rattle, even when my schedule seems to gallop ahead, out of my control.

But it will not run ahead of Another's watchful eye. So I hope in him.

Aching with Hope

Christ as a light,
  Illumine and guide me!
Christ, as a shield, o'ershadow and cover me!
Christ be under me! Christ be over me!
  Christ be beside me
  On left hand and right!
Christ be before me, behind me, about me!
Christ this day be within and without me! [17]

—PATRICK

I HAVE NOT FELT VERY EASTERY TODAY. You would hardly know that it is the morning after Resurrection Sunday.

Yesterday's celebration at church was vivid enough. Trumpetlike Easter lilies decked the altar and steps everywhere I looked. I joined forces with three hundred fellow congregants singing Handel's "Hallelujah" chorus. Between our voices and the brass ensemble, we made the rafters shake, I'm sure. The church I attend shows influences of charismatic renewal, so we sang lively contemporary tunes, too, driving numbers complete with guitar, and to the mild disdain of some of our older members, *drums.*

During the pastor's sermon (about Jesus appearing to his early followers after his death) I closed my eyes; for an instant my heart leapt at picturing what had happened: the wild hope stirring in the disciples when he appeared to them alive—all the jumble of confusion and joy. But from the moment the alarm jangled me awake this morning, I have felt vaguely unhappy. Easter's glories seem fainter, paler. I even feel depressed. I'm not sure why.

I have been traveling too much, I suppose, leading workshops, keeping long hours at my desk when I am home, finishing my book, helping to home school Micah. And Jill has seemed distant, absorbed in struggles at work, concerned (as am I) about chest pains she developed while hiking recently. I may be just worn down internally.

But *depression?* Am I perhaps just feeling sorry for myself?

Something else is happening inside, though, I realize as this morning gets rolling. I begin praying this prayer handed down through the ages with Saint Patrick's name attached, and a subterranean something stirs in me again. I chose it last week from a compilation of prayers knowing only that I wanted something to set the right tone for Easter week. I had no idea how much I would need it today, how I would ache to be infused with its radiant hope. What providence at work!

How I need your light, O Christ! Please be within me and without me.

∽

I learn that Patrick, the purported author, had his dark moments, too, for all the light saturating this prayer. We may picture a sunny man who miraculously drove snakes from Ireland and used a shamrock to teach pagans the Trinity. But the namesake for annual "St. Patty's" Day parades in Boston lived a life far removed from the pop culture clichés. There is more grit to him than most realize—certainly than *I* had realized. My history books paint a portrait of raw faithfulness.

When he was sixteen, Patrick's family's village in Britain was overrun and ravaged by Irish raiders. No wonder he would later pray with imagery snatched from the bloody battlefield. *Christ, as a shield, o'ershadow and cover me!* I can imagine the pandemonium and shrieks, the pleas for mercy. How shielded my suburban adolescence played out compared to his! How protected my life now!

The slavers carted off the trembling adolescent. They sold him eventually to a ruthless Irish warrior-chief, a man who decorated his compound with the heads of his opponents stuck atop sharp poles. Patrick had no choice but to live the miserable life of a solitary shepherd—often cold, hungry, thirsty, with almost no shred of hope for rescue. He felt great oppression. And I worry about having to manage my twenty-first-century life!

But Patrick found in his sorrow a spur to profound growth. He uncovered, as I struggle to do today, another meaning behind his difficulties. Stranded in the hills with the sheep, not seeing another human for months at a time, he began reaching out for something he sensed, vaguely at first, beyond his hurting heart. In his loneliness, Patrick thought, *Why not reach out and talk to God?* Who *else* was there to talk to?

And so he turned to a God to whom he had paid only lip service before. "I would look after the sheep and pray often during the day," he later wrote in his *Confession*. "The love of God and the fear of him grew in me more and more. And my faith grew and my spirit was so stirred up that in one day I would say as many as a hundred prayers, and at night nearly as many, even when I was staying out in the woods or on the mountain. Through snow and frost and rain I would rise before dawn for prayer."[18]

Is it any wonder I could find myself warming to the words of one who had weathered hard times, survived and thrived in circumstances far worse than mine? Beset with annoying, petty blues as I am, what better tonic could I find? In Patrick's words:

> At Tara today, in this awful hour,
> I call upon the Holy Trinity!
> Glory to him who reigneth in power,
> The God of the elements, Father and Son,
> And Paraclete Spirit, which Three are in One,
> The ever-existing Divinity![19]

∽

Yesterday's blues are giving way to a brighter view. I see how Patrick allowed his trouble to prompt him to prayer. I am trying to do that today. Perhaps I will regain a sense of how what I'm doing fits into some larger scheme. How can I not be affected by a glimpse of a God who reigns in Triune glory?

After six years of his bitter slavery, during one of the unbroken months of solitude and prayer, Patrick heard God say, "Soon you will return to your own country." On the strength of the promise, Patrick fled, negotiating two hundred rugged miles to the coast, where he found a ship bound for France willing to take him aboard. He made his way back to Britain, to his family. But he would not stay long.

God again broke into his plans. Once home he heard a call to return to Ireland. This time, though, not as a slave, but as an evangelist.

It would go well, as we know from history. But Patrick also met with hostility, even threats of death from those most threatened: the druids, priests of magic and privileged guardians of pagan knowledge. The title appended to his prayer, "Before Tara," suggests the conflict that swirled around Patrick's simple preaching. Some scholars doubt the authenticity of Patrick's authorship of this hymn, but this is the idea: Patrick was resolved to celebrate Easter, 433, near Tara, where the princes and nobles of the whole kingdom gathered. On Easter Eve:

[Patrick] pitched his tent, and made preparations for celebrating the festival of Easter, and accordingly lighted the Paschal fire about night-fall. It happened that at this very time the king . . . and the assembled princes were celebrating a religious festival in honor of the return of the sun to power and heat. Part of the ritual of this festival consisted in every fire being extinguished for some days previous, that all might be relighted from the sacred fire in the palace on a certain day, [at] the temple of Tmora, on Tara hill, which was kindled on a certain day, now near at hand. Twilight had settled over the great plain, and all men waited for the red flame to shoot up on Tara hill, a signal that the festival was begun, and that all might rekindle their hearth fires from the consecrated blaze.

But a spark shone out far away on the plain, from the tent of Patrick.[20]

The king, angry and accompanied by two pagan priests and a crowd, galloped up to Patrick's fire. Unless someone extinguished Patrick's unauthorized fire, the Druids warned, it would overpower their fires, and the displeased gods would bring down the kingdom. Patrick's very life appeared to be endangered, but the king demanded only that Patrick appear the next day and explain himself. "On Easter-day, therefore," the chronicler recounts, "[Patrick] preached before the king and his nobles, and strove with the captious objections of the Wise-men."[21]

King Laoghaire seems not to have been converted, the legend tells us, but some family members were, and Patrick gained the favor of at least some of the powerful chieftains. God had answered his prayer for help and protection during desperate times.

How much of all this actually happened? The story does not even appear until centuries after it was supposed to have occurred. Patrick himself breathes not a word of it—strange given how much he does tell us of his life in his *Confession*. But the showdown, Patrick's courage, and the prayer that supposedly arose in the thick of it, rings true in spirit, at least. And I find myself drawing in some of its unshakable confidence, reminded where to look for strength.

൭൭

The ending to Patrick's hymn points me in the right direction:

> *Salvation dwells with the Lord,*
> *With Christ, the omnipotent Word.*
> *From generation to generation*
> *Grant us, O Lord, thy grace and salvation!* [22]

I learn from one of Patrick's biographers of his evident humility. Patrick often felt vulnerable, even helpless. Being wrenched from his comfortable home while still a child may have been part of that. Even toward the end of his life, as an old man and venerable bishop, he refers to himself as a "poor ignorant orphan," as an "exile and refugee." He was also keenly conscious of gaps in his education occasioned by his captivity. In his *Confession* he repeatedly calls himself "uncultivated."

But I think his humility had even deeper roots: a sense that all he did and what he accomplished had to do with God's empowering presence. So in his *Confession* he attributed his evangelistic success in Ireland not to his abilities, but to the Unseen One present in his efforts. "I was like a stone lying in deep mud," he says, "and God who is mighty came and in his compassion raised me up and exalted me very high and placed me atop a wall; and therefore I am compelled to cry out to repay, at least in part, God's benefits, benefits that here are so great and that in eternity our minds cannot calculate."[23]

This is surely some of what Patrick learned, through hardship or success, through glory or controversy, through exalted joy or moments his spirit felt low. Easter, Patrick would tell us, has to do with a reality far beyond our shifting moods and fickle emotions.

ᘐ

My good intentions just collided with reality. It is toward the end of my week with Patrick's prayers. Earlier today I stood in a library and came across a review of a book on prayer I had written. The review not only had few kind things to say, but dismissed the entire intention of the book, the entire audience I was intending to reach. I could almost imagine the reviewer looking down her nose at the words while she read. It was discouraging, even embarrassing. I was dismayed.

I must, ultimately, as always, turn again to God.

> *At Tara today, in this awful hour,*
> *I call on the Holy Trinity!*

I should not complain, I know. I admit there was a germ of truth in the reviewer's criticism, if only a small germ. And sometimes when I look at my writing and ministry opportunities, I stand amazed. I'm doing what I only dreamed about doing just years ago. I must learn again that God graciously consents to use my small efforts. He shows up in my disappointments and triumphs and works through them all.

Glory to him who reigns in power, not glory to me! God is accomplishing *his* purposes, no matter how well or poorly my little efforts turn out. I want to submit to God, not waste my waking hours in ruffled feelings. I want to let my discouragement lead me to enjoy God's constant and sustaining encouragement, no matter my circumstances or feelings.

Poor in Spirit

God strengthen me to bear myself,
That heaviest weight of all to bear,
Inalienable weight of care. . . .
All others are outside myself;
I lock my door and bar them out,
The turmoil, tedium, gad-about. . . .
God harden me against myself,
This coward with pathetic voice
Who craves for ease, and rest, and joys.
Myself, arch-traitor to myself,
My hollowest friend, my deadliest foe,
My clog whatever road I go.
Yet one there is can curb myself,
Can roll the strangling load from me,
Break off the yoke and set me free.[24]

—CHRISTINA ROSSETTI

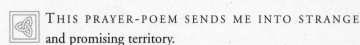

THIS PRAYER-POEM SENDS ME INTO STRANGE
and promising territory.

As I pray it this morning, at first it strikes me as odd to consider myself a heavy load. This is not how I tend to think about
me. *The heaviest of all?* Not in this day that encourages me to
make self-fulfillment the ultimate goal. Not in a culture that tells

me to guard my cafeteria tray of hoarded wants as an unquestioned good. Not during an era where "I've gotta be me" is my sacred due, doing "my own thing" an idol. These have been the goals my culture has suckled me on: self-gratification, self-esteem, even self-indulgence. After all, I am told, I deserve it!

And yet here I find myself praying, *God strengthen me to bear myself . . . Inalienable weight of care. . . . Break off the yoke*. Later, I find, the version of Rosetti's poem I used omitted a stanza that underlines this severe view even more:

> *I lock my door upon myself.*
> *And bar them out; but who shall wall*
> *Self from myself, most loathed of all?*

Most loathed of all? Me? I think I know what Rossetti is getting at, though. My glimmering awareness came to me as a two-part question: Why do I take my worries so seriously? And why do I take the weighty assurances of my faith so lightly?

How much trouble I have this morning getting out of my mind the disappointing mention of my book in the review yesterday. Even while I sit to pray I find myself obsessing again. I rehearse my comebacks to a review-writer I will never meet, plot my letter of self-justifying revenge to the editors. I can't seem to shake my alternating sadness and anger.

And I see how self-involved I am at root. I realize again why the phrase *self-conscious* usually carries a negative ring—a person hampered or made awkward or pulled down by too much of him- or herself. But how can I move beyond it? There is precious little in me that is *un*self-conscious. That lives with unstudied disregard for others' opinions of me or what I do. How addicted I seem to my self's demands for attention and approval!

So I stick with Rossetti's prayer. Maybe it goes too far. But then usually I don't go far enough.

༄

Perhaps Rossetti's recurring turn to self-renunciation accounts for her dwindling popularity in our day of self-worship. In the days of nineteenth-century Victorian England, she reigned as the beloved, perhaps even the leading, female poet. Some consider her among the greatest religious poets in the English language. Her name comes up now mostly among literature scholars, or through the poem that became a Christmas carol: "In the Bleak Midwinter." But her star has faded from the literary universe. One professor and critic offers this reason: While she was loved for the "clarity and sweetness of her diction," he says, "for her realistic imagery, and for the purity of her faith," she now reads as quaint. "Perhaps the simplicity of Christina Rossetti's faith seems remote and unrealistic to many contemporary readers," he concludes.[25]

Perhaps her decline also has to do with her sense of the self as something not to be pampered. She saw, as C. S. Lewis would put it in the next century, that people are not sufficient for their own bliss. Not a message that plays well in our desperately self-seeking age.

༄

A part of me knows such sentiments can be overdone, of course. As I pray the prayer this morning, I realize that renunciation and criticism of self, in an odd, old paradox, can become yet her way to focus on self. Rossetti, I learn, lived her life unsure that she would be among those chosen for salvation on Judgment Day.

Worries about the state of her own soul distracted and plagued her.

Perhaps Rossetti's forceful will had something to do with her fears about indulging her needs and wants. From her infancy, friends and family spoke of a Christina who was feisty, possessed of a fiery temper. Her father called her his "angelic little demon" (a terrible nickname for a child!). Once, when scolded by her mother, she took a pair of scissors and cut and ripped up her own arm, getting back at her parents even if it meant harming herself.

Did her self-flagellation as an adult carry a similarly self-centered ring? Her poetry often focused on giving up pleasure and enduring unrequited love (she never married, despite two proposals, declining the men's invitations because she questioned the depth of their faith). She battled heart disease and tuberculosis for so many years that her brother once said that she was compelled to view life itself as "a valley of the shadow of death."

Does this maudlin, dreary outlook really point me to God? Or simply give me another reason to fixate on myself?

∽

But then I read a prayer of Thomas Merton's in the second volume of his journals, *Entering the Silence,* a prayer that helps me make sense of the dilemma. This is how he prays:

O Lord! How joyful and happy must they be, who, when they come to consider their own selves, find in themselves nothing remarkable whatever. Not only do they attract no attention outside themselves, but now they no longer have any desire or selfish desires to attract their own attention. They remark no virtues, they are saddened by no huge sins, they see only their own unremarkable weakness . . . which is filled, obscurely, not with themselves but with your love, O God! They are the poor in spirit, who possess within themselves the kingdom of heaven because they are no longer remarkable even to themselves, but in them shines God's light, and they themselves and all who see it glorify you, O God!"[26]

And I think, *Here is how it all falls into place:* I learn to live without undue focus on my gifts and needs, and yet without an overblown fascination with my failings. I try not to get bogged down in myself, yet don't get bogged down in guilt over my getting bogged down, either. I make my focus not my self, but on God's Self. Not on my little world of advances and fallings short, but on the expansive, glorious realm of a gracious, unfathomable God. I admit my weakness, as Merton helped me to do, but realize the way through is to let God fill me with his love. I swear off harassing myself about my littleness and instead fix my gaze on God's bigness.

It is right, then, to pray, as Rossetti does, that God will free me from myself, break the yoke, lead me to liberty.

I don't knock myself out worrying. I try to love God, put my focus there, and believe that out of that new way of looking at things, my self will take its proper place. It will make itself known, not to nag, but to help me become all God wants me to be. Not just for my own self, my own sake, but for others' as well.

Thy Kingdom Come

Our Father which art in heaven,
Hallowed be thy name.
Thy kingdom come.
Thy will be done in earth,
  as it is in heaven.
Give us this day our daily bread.
And forgive us our debts,
  as we forgive our debtors.
And lead us not into temptation,
  but deliver us from evil:
For thine is the kingdom,
  and the power,
  and the glory,
  forever.
Amen.

—JESUS

IT IS GOOD I AM FOCUSING ON THIS PRAYER this week, a prayer I can easily call to memory from Matthew's Gospel. I was awakened at a dark hour this morning when Rascal, our tiny mixed terrier-hound, whimpered that he needed to be let outside. Once in bed again, I couldn't go back to sleep.

I found myself troubled by the scenes of the day past—especially a TV news account of a man who, on a live broadcast in Los Angeles, sent shards of his skull and brain spewing across the pavement through a self-inflicted shotgun blast. Even my mental pictures of Jesus, as I reached out to pray, seemed skewed and distorted. It was all middle-of-the-night weirdness, I suppose. Soon I found myself forming the words to this prayer. I turned to God knowing the only cure for my haunted wakefulness was somehow found in God. *Our Father, who art in heaven.* . . . Just affirming something simple yet profound about God helped me grow less disturbed. I drifted off to sleep.

I don't remember when I first learned this prayer in Matthew 6:9–13 (KJV). I don't think my mother, the one who prayed the most in our house, sat me down to memorize it. But growing up in a believing household, going to church Sunday mornings in the Methodist Church, I heard its familiar phrases and rhythms from my earliest days. How much did I understand phrases like *hallowed be thy name, . . . thy kingdom come, . . . forgive us our debts?* I cannot recall. Only later did their full import strike me, help me, and motivate me. But their majestic assurance seeped into my young consciousness. Surely the words shaped me in hidden and unseen ways and account for much of what I now know and believe and trust.

ço

Another day. The oddest thing has been happening in my praying. I intend to start out saying, *Our Father, who art in heaven.* But I find myself repeating instead, *The Lord is my shepherd,* the opening line of the twenty-third psalm. And then I realize what I'm doing and start over, this time consciously saying, *Our Father.* . . . So even though I start to pray one way, some old habit kicks in. I have more vivid memories crowding around the psalm, the one that I can most clearly remember my mother reciting when I was a child of eight or nine.

But this is no accident, I decide.

Both shepherds and fathers, in ancient times as well as now, wielded impressive authority tempered by tender care. So the prophet Isaiah said of God:

> He tends his flock like a shepherd:
> He gathers the lambs in his arms
>   and carries them close to his heart;
> he gently leads those that have young (Isaiah 40:11).

"The green pastures" of Psalm 23 become a metaphor for all that makes life flourish and grow. The "still waters" to which a shepherd leads his flock promise rest and relief for what troubles us, just as parental love at its best will nourish us and help us grow. Much of this is captured for me, I decide, in calling God *Father.*

❦

Later in the week, driving to pick up my son from his home-school tutorial, my mind jumping from project to project, my thoughts rambling about a decision I need to make about my part-time job, my curiosity about ordination growing, I find myself praying, *Thy kingdom come. Thy will be done.* The phrases came naturally, easily. I feel my agitation melt.

It was an act of will, of course, to commit my racing thoughts to God. But more than anything, a relief. Who better to manage the affairs that concern me? Why not let God's will have sway, move aside and let God have his way? Why not long for his kingdom, what some translate as the *rule of God,* to prevail amid our world's petty kingdoms of little selves?

And then I find myself drawn to the phrase, *in earth as it is in heaven.* I want life to be more than it is, more like what it can be. Much I do not grasp about heaven, but what I know makes me yearn for it to be real, more real than it is, more present than it seems to be now. There is a boldness to this phrase—indeed, all these phrases—that makes this one more like a shout and an imperative than a wimpy wish. Because this is a prayer to a vigorous God, the prayer itself becomes more vigorous.

The very structure of this prayer helps me remember not to treat these matters casually, lazily. The opening words lay clear accent on the One addressed. Prayer, according to this way of praying Jesus taught his disciples, begins with acknowledging the God we approach. It gives God proper place. The first three of the six petitions—half of the prayer!—begin with God and his agenda, not mine. I am reminded about far larger concerns, a wonderfully vaster panorama, before I even think about my own need for daily bread or forgiveness or deliverance. I hold sacred the name of God. Even the faintest, fleeting thought of him I honor. And I turn this Godward focus into bold petitions.

෴

When I was a pastor in rural Virginia, I would occasionally include the Lord's Prayer in the printed order of worship we used every Sunday. One member cautioned me: "Don't repeat it too often. If we say it over and over it will lose its freshness. It will become meaningless." She implied that she felt familiarity breeds indifference. I didn't agree with her, at least not fully, but I ended up following her advice to some extent. To my regret now, I found myself hesitating to use this powerful prayer in the services.

But now I believe that this prayer bears well under repeated utterance. Far from losing its vividness with repetition, it grows richer and richer. It takes on more and more meaning. I have written about it before, but manage never to run out of things to say. It gains in power and energy with my soul's repeated fingering of its phrases and movements. I think of Martin Luther, the courageous, feisty church reformer from the sixteenth century: "To this day," he once wrote, "I am still nursing myself on the Lord's Prayer like a child and am still eating and drinking of it like an old man without getting bored with it."[27]

So it happens for me, too, in the sleepless watches of a restless night, or in the bright day of active plans and expansive ambitions. Constantly I come back to the center of prayer: wanting done the will of my heavenly Father. And surely it will be done. *Thy kingdom come.*

Be Still

May God shelter me,
May God shepherd me.
May God strengthen me,
And go with me wherever I go.[28]
—CELTIC TRADITION (ADAPTED)

THIS WEEK HOLDS AN INTRIGUING, EVEN risky experiment for me. And this ancient prayer from the Celtic tradition, from people living on the fringes and isles of Britain from ancient times, is helping me keep at it.

Especially this morning. I've been working on talks for a retreat I am to lead for campus pastors from around the state. As I awoke I knew I would have to make long strides of progress by the end of the day, with only a few hours left before the weekend. I needed to flex my fingers, boot up my computer, and work.

But I also began feeling keenly my lack of prayer. A friend had called before I got out the door for my morning run and prayer time, a friend struggling through a painful church conflict. Of course I stayed put and listened. And then, with some of the morning already gone, I had to ask, *What should I give priority to?* My sense of responsibility said to sit down and work.

But I made the illogical choice. I went on my run instead. And as I ran, praying all the way, asking for God to shield my life and keep his eye on me, something striking happened: ideas for things to say during the retreat crowded into the space opened for him. Insights flowed so quickly that within minutes I had mentally roughed out a whole block of my talks.

I came in from my run, had a bowl of Special K, looked at the kitchen clock, and noticed that it was after 10:00. But instead of panicking I had a satisfying feeling of having "done" a lot already. After my shower, by the time I sat down to work, I had much to say. I had been *given* much to say. I encountered again the paradox of doing by not doing, accomplishing by not striving, finding my words by protecting quiet. I am convinced that I got more done than I otherwise could have by my contemplative inaction, by my stilling myself mentally, by my needy opening to Another. And who knows how much more fruitful my time with those wearied, burdened campus workers turned out for my having chosen prayer over my own self-propelled, agitated activity.

Indeed, much of what I would eventually share with those gathered at the retreat focused on where any of us gains insight and energy to do what God calls us to do. The temptation is to place greatest weight on the things we think must get done, rather than on the means, the energy, and the divine power that enables us to get them done.

And so, I realized, preaching to myself as I tapped out my ideas on the computer, we operate out of several sources. Such as agitation. That feeling inside that something around us must be fixed, preferably right away. Agitation has great power to motivate us. And there is a place for a kind of healthy agitation, at least sometimes. As when we see a need—we feel a tug to respond and so we do. But often—more often than not—our urgency is of a different sort. Someone or some situation, we think, cannot get by without what we can do. We rush in to help without asking whether or how we should. We think, grandiosely, that the most powerful tool of change is our own effort. Our eloquence. Our intelligence. We're ready for action! But we find little peace. We feel driven.

And by all means we never sit still. We don't pause to hear the mind of God. We forget to start with God's prior invitation to "Be still, and know that I am God" (Psalm 46:10). Our agitation pushes us to a fair amount of exertion, but what we do as a result often lacks true power. Agitation rarely guides us to what we should do next. But it always gives us a reason to pray.

∽

Related to agitation, but slightly different, is the temptation to turn activity into activism, our responsibility into overblown urgency. But mere activism can never long support ministry either. It eventually gives out because it is not a renewable resource. It uses itself up. We end up depleted.

Certainly Christian faith has a great deal to do with doing. Jesus went about *doing* good, Acts reminds us. But we tend merely to *go about*. At least I do. For Jesus, however, all he did grew out of an intimate relationship with God. So even though a swirl of motion and need often greeted him, what he did flowed from a different spring.

For amid all the activity of Jesus' ministry, still, we see, "very early in the morning, while it was still dark, Jesus got up, left the house and went to a solitary place, where he prayed" (Mark 1:35). Locked within the loud words of activity and temptation to agitation is a simple verse that points to the quiet communion that fed Jesus' ministry, and that promises to feed ours as well.

Which leads to the third, more viable source of right action. Attentiveness. Intimacy with God. Only when we carve out spaces of stillness in which to listen to him can we adequately respond to the clamor of need and opportunity all around us. Only then will our concern for reform be more than striving. Only when we are open to God, the source of all power, will we have what it takes to do more than merely do.

҈

For all the impact of my discoveries, this has ended up a tough week for praying. For some reason, this week I have found myself resisting the very idea of praying another's prayer. I feel all this even though I love the tone and sentiment of this prayer with roots in the European people who shared a family of languages represented by Gaelic, Irish, and Welsh. The Celts were known for their emphasis on the availability of God, smack in the midst of daily life. They knew that creation and everyday work, not just church buildings, could become a place of prayer. *But why bother with this form,* I think, *when I can simply sit in God's presence unencumbered by another's words?*

But then, later this morning, riding in the car on a spring day flooded with brilliant sunshine while my son Micah and I carpooled, I thought of the phrase, *May God shelter me.* Suddenly it became *my* prayer, one I might not have thought up on my own but that nevertheless I needed to pray. The words helped me invite God to come into my little concerns and overshadow them with his goodness. And now I think how good it is to know that God is watching me, loving me, caring for me. As the prophet said so long ago: "O God, you will keep in perfect peace those whose minds are fixed on you; for in returning and rest we shall be saved; in quietness and trust shall be our strength" (Isaiah 26:3; 30:15).

I want my days to have some of the very quality of heaven

about them, as daunting as that seems some days. So I keep praying for peace. But I also just try to sit still. Sometimes that is the great accomplishment. In a recent Gallup Poll 64 percent of respondents, when asked how they prayed, said that they "sit quietly and just think about God." That is not *all* there is to prayer, of course. But such resting in the source of peace and the presence of good has great impact on my soul. It equips me far more than my frantic busyness, my insistence that I make progress in the Christian life by being more ingenious or energetic.

෧෧

I recall the season of the church calendar we are in, for Christians who follow such matters: the season of Easter, the echoes of resurrection proclamations still echoing in our hearts. And I think of a verse that has long intrigued me. In Ephesians, Paul said that the power working in us and in what we do is the same power that God "exerted in Christ when he raised him from the dead and seated him at his right hand in the heavenly realms" (Ephesians 1:20). I find that an astonishing promise, but one I will miss experiencing if I focus only on my own effort.

More than any mere activity I can offer, I need to think about the larger, deeper resources that are ever-available. I need to let them come flowing in.

> *May God strengthen me,*
> *And go with me wherever I go.*

Thirsting for God

O God, you are my God,
earnestly I seek you;
my soul thirsts for you,
my body longs for you,
in a dry and weary land
where there is no water.

—DAVID, THE PSALMIST

YESTERDAY, AT THE RETREAT OF CAMPUS ministers I led, during a blisteringly hot Tennessee afternoon, I had the group spend some time with David's prayer from Psalm 63:1. I said that I would stop talking and let them walk the grounds or sit quietly in the shade of the cabin porch or stay in their seats. But however you do it, I said, meditate on this verse and make it your own prayer. Let its longing for God express yours.

We reassembled after twenty minutes or so to reflect on our time with the verse. One burly man with a booming voice confessed, "I feel like a liar." He certainly got our attention. "I prayed this verse," he went on, "but I have to admit that I don't *thirst* for God. I can't really say I long for God with my body and soul."

There came a poignant pause; this was sharing not to be glibly cluttered with talk. Finally I thanked him for his honesty, and then I mentioned how the Bible sometimes puts before us a mirror; how when we look at ourselves reflected back, we may see failings or blemishes. But, I said, we also can pray our way "into" the reality of such verses. We pray even when the sentiment does not flow effortlessly from deep wellsprings of the soul. A prayer such as this can help us precisely at such times. We can let its conviction or intensity infuse our lackluster seeking.

I have to admit, like the honest member of our group, that I, too, sometimes find my spiritual thirst getting buried under my routine. I don't always pay it the attention I could or should. I just go along.

Then something happens to make me aware again. Perhaps a disruption in my routine. Or some disappointment. A hardship strips away my complacency.

I think of something Jewish storyteller Isaac Singer once said. "I only pray when I'm in trouble," he wrote, with what must have been a twinkle in his eye, "but since I'm in trouble all the time, I pray all the time."[29] And just as a withering hot late-May sun, such as we felt during our retreat, makes us keenly aware of our thirst, so do life's difficulties. So does my inner yearning for water for my cracked, neglected soul.

I mentioned to the group how the psalm grew precisely out of such need. How thirst is a key component of spiritual growth. My Bible heads Psalm 63 with a title:

"A psalm of David. When he was in the Desert of Judah."

Some say perhaps the verses (and the title) allude to the time when David, fleeing Absalom and his treachery, grows faint and "weary" in the wilderness (1 Samuel 16:2, 14). The notation about the setting applies even if a skeptic would not place the psalm in the deserts of a Semitic king's life. Who cannot picture a parched, heavy-footed, heat-dazed traveler making his or her way across arid sands or rocky cliffs? And not recall times when the life of faith seemed just as dry and stumblingly hard?

The word *seek* here is not, in the original language, the usual word, scholars tell us; no, this one is much more intense, earnest, desperate. And it is related to the Hebrew word for "dawn," suggesting a seeking that begins from the moment of awaking, from the earliest light. The psalm writer aches for God, and yet does not despair, believing fully that God, *"my* God," he says, does not appear as some mirage, but ultimately as a thirst-slaking reality.

∽

Once again, I find a prayer from another helping me to speak to God "out of the depths," to recall the words of another psalm (130). I find the words of someone who lived long before me prompting mine. Reminding me, when I might simply go thirsty, that my thirst will take me somewhere verdant and refreshing, if I let it, if I bother to notice it. Reminding me that a dry and weary land is not my permanent residence. Not if I keep traveling, keep thirsting for God.

Getting Out of Myself

*Almighty God our heavenly Father, you declare your glory
and show forth your handiwork in the heavens and in the
earth: Deliver us in our various occupations from the service
of self alone, that we may do the work you give us to do in
truth and beauty and for the common good; for the sake of
him who came among us as one who serves, your Son Jesus
Christ our Lord, who lives and reigns with you and the Holy
Spirit, one God, for ever and ever.*
—THE BOOK OF COMMON PRAYER

THIS WEEK I FIND MYSELF THINKING ABOUT
the God I pray to—a God I hope can lift my life out of its dol-
drums, a magnificent Creator and Sustainer who can pry my eyes away
from too-small realities. I want to take in a larger panorama. I *need* to.
This prayer is helping me see what I otherwise might have missed.

I take a minute to pray it while on a break at work. I've poured
a cup of coffee that I hope will help me stay alert through the
afternoon of tasks piling up on my desk: slips of paper with the
phone numbers of people to call, a meeting agenda to prepare, a
legal document to review. I have trouble mustering any enthusiasm. I find myself daydreaming (I should say *fantasizing*) about
what I wish I were doing instead. The work before me seems so
mundane, my world so little, my accomplishments so meager. But

before I get back to it all, I pull out my prayer for the week.

As I read it, the words open up another world to me. Even before any petition, before anything gets asked (and I have plenty to unload on God right now), the prayer has me remembering God as *Almighty* and a *heavenly Father.* It is no accident that many of the prayers in this book of "common" (as in corporate, not mundane) prayers begin with an ascription of praise or a statement about God's character. How frequently do my own free-lance, off-the-cuff prayers leave me mostly entertaining my own wants and imagined needs. How tempting to recite my desires with barely a thought of acknowledging the God I pray to. But to ponder God himself! What, when I stop to think about it, could be more fascinating?

I recall a book, *Celebration of Praise,* that years ago revolutionized my understanding of prayer. But sometimes I still forget its message. The author, Dick Eastman, wrote of a discovery, one I need constantly to relearn: how crucial it is to live cognizant of great truths about God's nature and character, his infinite immensity, his unfathomable goodness. "The highest science," Eastman quoted nineteenth-century preacher Charles Spurgeon as saying, "the loftiest speculation, the mightiest philosophy that can ever engage the attention of the child of God is the name, the nature, the person, the work, the doings, and the existence of the great God whom he calls Father."[30]

Sometimes I'm tempted to believe that what brings me down has to do with the circumstances of my life: a conflict with a family member, lists of grungy job tasks, lack of being noticed by those whose attention I crave. But in my clearer moments I realize that my outlook has to do with something far deeper, much higher. It hinges instead on my answer to the question, *Who lies at the foundation of all that has been and will be?* Would that I meditated on the One above all thoughts for even a fraction of the time I spend thinking about me! Charles Spurgeon told the congregation in New Park Street Chapel in England so long ago that nothing can "so comfort the soul, . . . so speak peace to the winds of trial, as a devout musing on the subject of the Godhead."[31]

The language is archaic, but the thought appealing. I get constant reminders, signs, pointers, this prayer tells me. *You declare your glory and show forth your handiwork in the heavens and in the earth.* This is not a God who absents himself from daily life. He shows up and leaves traces. He writes a flourishing signature on all that is, letting us see his glory.

Thomas Merton talks about the world being transparent to the presence and glory of God. But still we miss it. "According to the great mystics within [the Western spiritual tradition]," writes spiritual teacher Ronald Rolheiser, "we generally lack the purity of heart necessary to see God because normal awareness is both very reduced and muddied by unhealthy self-concern, excessive preoccupation with our own agendas, and with restless distractions. God is present but we are, for the most part, asleep, distracted, and unaware of that presence."[32]

But still I get glimmers. I see enough—most of us see enough—that it makes us want to know more. "If the doors of perception were cleansed, everything would appear to humankind as it is, infinite," said William Blake, the eccentric philosopher-poet and artist.[33] It is said that once he heard some "persons of a scientific bent once discoursing pompously . . . about the incredible distance of the planets, the length of time light takes to travel to the earth, . . . when he burst out, 'Tis false! I was walking down a lane the other day, and at the end of it I touched the sky with my stick.'"[34]

We can almost touch God, or at least listen for him, through the world he has made. As the psalmist proclaims,

The heavens declare the glory of God;
the skies proclaim the work of his hands.
Day after day they pour forth speech;
night after night they display knowledge.
There is no speech or language
where their voice is not heard (Psalm 19:1–3).

∽

So I ask for divine help to do my work "in truth and beauty." And to think outside my narrow confines of self-interest. I want to live more "for the common good." There is a larger scheme, a fuller meaning beyond just the things I have to do.

To be *delivered from the service of self alone,* that is part of it. And so I remind myself that what I do does not have always to leave me feeling thrillingly fulfilled. Not when I realize that what I am doing, day-in and day-out, purchases the walls and roof that protect my family from cold and sweltering heat. Not when I realize that irritating administrative details, as well as exhilarating triumphs, will produce a product that someone will use, perhaps even treasure. I can let myself be lifted out of myself and recognize that we are all in this together. And I can glimpse again the wildly wonderful God I claim to serve. I call to mind the great Father of vast power and incomprehensible glory.

But my prayer this week does not end on this exultant note. It returns my focus again to the servant Son, this holy One who allowed himself to be reduced to ordinariness, coming not only as one who lives and reigns, but as one who serves. Who washes sweaty, dusty feet. Who stretches out his arms on a cross to suffer, even die, losing himself so that we can find him. And be found, wherever we are.

Opening Doors Instead of Building Walls

Sweet Lord, have patience with us. We build walls that divide. We close doors to keep others out. Teach us how to topple the walls stone by stone. Show us how to open the doors and bless all who enter. [35]

—CHRISTOPHER DE VINCK

I HAD LUNCH YESTERDAY AT A LOCAL MEXICAN cafe with a colleague, and something about our time unsettles me.

It was our third time to meet over lunch. His lanky frame, unusual for a middle-aged man, towers above me—I who am already tall. But his gentle voice never overpowers. While we ate, I realized again how much I enjoy Thomas's kind spirit. We talked about the normal office stresses, our families. And while we come from very different church backgrounds, we ask many of the same questions: *How do I truly live what I believe? How do I make time for God in a busy schedule?*

As we walked back to our offices, Thomas said, "I find these times refreshing. Maybe we should make them semi-regular."

Of course I said yes. Eagerly. We got out our date books and set up another lunch.

And yet, as I say, something nagged at me when we parted. As I reflected on our conversation, I realized that I had inwardly found fault with little things Thomas had said, with views slightly different from my own. Maybe it was no more than afternoon crankiness. But here I was spending time with someone who was becoming a special friend, and I was feeling uncharitable. For no real reason.

Today, as I pray, I suspect much of my nagging irritation had to do with my tendency to build walls in relationships. I do it in far worse ways with others, especially people who seem vastly different from me. Such pettiness arises from the temptation to keep others at arm's length, even people I like, and especially people I don't. Finding little things to pick at helps me keep myself apart. If I can criticize another, some part of me reasons, I occupy some superior place. If I look down, I must be above and better. But doing so, whether out of bad habit or a desire to avoid personal injury, distracts me from focusing gratefully on the gift another can be.

So I turn to de Vinck's little prayer, passed along to me by a friend on the Internet. Chris is a writer I admire, whose book about his severely disabled brother, *The Power of the Powerless,* ministers to me still. Chris has himself become a friend after we met at a writer's conference. So I let his prayer remind me to ask God for help in not building yet more walls. I want to make my life more hospitable to friends. I want to give less of an ear to the nagging voices of habitual criticism of those I do not naturally embrace. I don't want to close the door to keep another away. For I do it too much, too often. I guard myself too carefully.

I want a different way.

☙

Later in the week, God seems to be placing in front of me reminders of my good intentions.

Like tonight. I usually read in bed just before clicking off my light. I'm deep into a mystery by Ellis Peters which revolves around an eleventh-century monk named Brother Cadfael. Someone once called the almost two-dozen books in the Peters series "medieval whodunits," and they strike me by turns as entertaining and profound. And now, in my reading, I have come across an encounter that reminds me yet again of the persistent power that holds us back, apart, tight.

Here is what happens in the book: Brother Cadfael finds himself seated at breakfast next to a new monk in the abbey, Brother Eutropius, who had been in the monastery only two months. While Brother Oswin, a favorite of Cadfael's, "would have been an open book to every reader" by that time, Cadfael muses, Eutropius "contained himself as tightly as did his skin, and gave out much less in the way of information." Still, thinks Cadfael, "some day someone would pierce that carapace of his, with an unguarded word or a sudden irresistible motion of grace, and the mystery would no longer be a mystery, or the stranger a stranger. Brother Cadfael knew better than to be in a hurry, where souls were concerned. There was plenty of elbow room in eternity."[36] And Cadfael was right, I find as the story unfolds.

I don't hold myself quite so tightly as Brother Eutropius, I think. But still, how I need people or events to pierce my carapace! I need a work of grace to help me crack open the shell of my well-protected heart.

Show us how to open the doors and bless all who enter.

∾

This prayer makes me think of a larger way, a bigger context, in which I need to pray. Just weeks ago I volunteered for Saturday night duty at my church, for our slot in a community-wide program called

Room in the Inn, an interfaith effort of Nashville churches and synagogues. More than a hundred churches open their doors to provide food and shelter on a rotating basis for two hundred homeless people during the cold months.

I was on duty with Jim Pichert, the director of our congregation's work with the program. Jim and I both arrived a bit frazzled that evening. We had had hectic Saturdays. And we knew that these dozen homeless people, with their odd smells and peculiar dress, would require our patience. After supper was served and dishes cleared away, however, we began to feel camaraderie with our guests. Most of us watched an NCAA basketball playoff game well into the evening, occupying hard folding chairs under the florescent harsh light of our church's parish hall. Homeless people usually long for bed early, however, and soon they were settled into their cots, deeply asleep.

The next morning, not long after dawn, Jim and I each rounded up a carload of guests to drive them back to the converted downtown warehouse that serves as the program's hub. On the way, listening to their banter, I heard unadorned vignettes about the brute realities of street life. After we dropped them off and Jim and I got ready to go back to the church, he asked, "Have you ever been inside the building?" He wanted to introduce me to the regular volunteers.

In we went, between the parking lot and the three-story building, threading through a fenced-in rectangle of the parking lot. It looked to be a kind of meeting place and waiting area. Scores of homeless people milled around, some waiting to go to a day job, some talking to friends and pulling long draws on cigarettes. I'm sure almost all wondered where they would spend the day—and sleep that night. It was an incredible cross-section of humanity— all sizes, shapes, colors, ages—even one older woman, I remember, in a wheel chair. *To sit in a wheel chair* and *be homeless!* I thought.

And suddenly, as I looked at the crowd—raggedly dressed, faces creased and bronzed from sun, mouths full of stained and rotting teeth—an instant sense of the presence of Christ washed over me, radiating from the seamy crowd in front of me. The sensation caught me unawares, rolling over me like a wave. Through this remnant of broken humanity Christ was mediating himself to me. I felt great love. "The sunshine," I wrote in my journal, "seemed to bathe the scene with a kind of divine sweetness."

My walls were down. I wasn't thinking with disgust about the people's smell or devising plans to rehabilitate them. Not only was I in that moment not apart, not somehow above these folks, I was met by Christ himself *among them.* And I felt his presence more vividly than I would in church later that morning.

Teach us how to topple the walls stone by stone. Show us how to open the doors and bless all who enter. By a grace beyond me, God was answering my prayer, showing up in these forlorn specimens of cast-off humanity that I would never otherwise spend much attention on. I thought of the text in Matthew where Jesus said as you've done it to "the least of these brothers of mine"—the poor and sick and imprisoned—you've done it also "for me" (Matthew 25:40). Always before I heard that statement as a duty, a responsibility. Now I received it also as a promise.

These glimpses come as rare gifts, I know. But even when we aren't privileged with dramatic experiences, I see today that God draws near in and through others. *Why keep people,* I tell myself—*friends, family, even antagonists—at a distance when untold things can happen when I let them close?* And I turn my resolve into prayer, knowing the old patterns will die hard.

May I let them in, O Lord. Show me how to open the doors and bless all who enter.

The One Who Knows Me Best

O Lord, you have searched me and known me.
You know when I sit down and when I rise up;
* you discern my thoughts from far away.*
You search out my path and my lying down,
* and are acquainted with all my ways.*
Even before a word is on my tongue,
* O Lord, you know it completely.*
You hem me in, behind and before,
* and lay your hand upon me.*
Such knowledge is too wonderful for me,
* it is so high that I cannot attain it.*

—DAVID, THE PSALMIST

FOR ALL THE TIMES I HAVE READ OR HEARD Psalm 139:1–6, I have yet to let its unfathomably astonishing truth fully grab my imagination. *How I am known!* I am noticed with unbelievably intimate intricacy.

I am known in many ways, both mundane and profound, of course. I was known by my parents (both now deceased). I was known as a baby with cooing smiles, a toddler with wobbly steps, an alert, eager-to-please child, a thoughtful adolescent, an ambitious young man. My dad never saw me hit middle adulthood, and my mom just barely. But they knew things about me instinctively, deeply.

And some things about me they thought they knew, but did not.

I am known intimately by my wife, who just the other day said, comparing my age with our anniversary, "Do you realize you have been married for as long as you were not married?" Sure enough, our wedding comes at a kind of midpoint in my forty-three years. Jill knows me better than anyone—she knows my hopes and secrets, my eyes and subtle gestures, my laughter and hurts.

I am known by others, too, of course. My children know me in a different way than Jill does, but they can still predict my reactions. They know my dreams and my embarrassments.

Knowing me less still, but well enough, is a close friend, Kevin. For a dozen years we have been confidants and prayer partners. Then there are newer friends like Chris, John, James, Hunter. I know another couple old enough to be my parents, Gwyn and Mary Lee, to whom I go when I need support and intercessory prayer. Their knowledge ranges from my love of pecan pie to my longings to nurture the prayer lives of others.

But none of this approaches God's knowledge of me. While many think of God as aloof and out of reach, this psalm, to my astonishment, tells me God knows me best of all. Of whom else, *to* whom else, can I say,

> You know when I sit down and when I rise up;
> you discern my thoughts from far away.
> You search out my path and my lying down,
> and are acquainted with all my ways.

Who else even comes close to such intimate foreknowledge, such present-tense attention, such circumspect awareness of all the places I have been, the commitments I have made, the temptations I have fallen for?

Even before a word is on my tongue,
O Lord, you know it completely.

No wonder King David stands in awe of God's piercing, confidential knowledge of his every thought and move. A vast, eternal God, tracing the little details of a man's fleeting life! Who would have dreamt it?

The glorious truth is that I have nothing to hide, as C. S. Lewis's prayer about the prayer preceding all prayers reminded me earlier in this year of praying. Nothing will be a surprise to God! How freeing!

෨

But I notice something else, too: To be known so intimately can sometimes make me draw back. Reid Cooper, who attends an adult Sunday school class I'm teaching, asked on a recent Sunday: "Do you think that we fear intimacy with God? That that's one reason we hold back in prayer sometimes?"

Of course. "What a profound point," I answered.

When a person knows us, he or she has some power over us. We lose some control of our self-protective schemes and strategies. Intimacy leaves us a bit unsettled, at least sometimes. We fear that God's knowledge of us, especially, will not be simply a passive thing, something that leaves us untouched, unscathed, but something that will change us. We fear that being known that intimately will inevitably affect our fiercely guarded individuality or interfere with our personal freedom. But only if we somehow think that we know better who we are, what we must have, where we are going.

One woman tells of her son's discomfort about all this:

Some years ago when my children were small, we were living in the [American] Southwest. A friend of ours gave us a huge *Ojo de Dios* (Eye of God) [a Native-American artifact] to hang on our wall. It was the largest one I had ever seen, measuring perhaps three feet tall and three feet wide. Since the color scheme used in the *ojo* was compatible with the colors in my oldest son's room, I hung it there over his bed. It remained there for several days without much being said about it. Finally one day, Mark came to me and said, 'Mom, please take that *ojo* out of my room. I don't want God seeing everything that I do.'

The mother, Betty Shannon Cloyd, remarks, "I realized that I had some work to do with his concept of God. He needed to understand that God is more like a tender shepherd who cares for us than a God who is out to get us for any little infraction of the rules. Although God knows what we do, God loves us anyway."[37]

Betty is right to ensure her son understands God's goodness. Still, for all her concern to reassure, it is unlikely that her child will ever completely lose the unsettling sense of the awesomeness of a God who knows us better than we know ourselves.

᪣

I read an article in yesterday's paper about male mid-life crises. I found, to no surprise, that I am smack in the middle of the prime age range. My back hurts more. My bones ache in ways they never did five years ago. My stomach, for all my morning jogging, continues to increase its girth. I feel quite middle-aged. And I think in light of that I am asking questions about the "bigger picture." There is a kind of winnowing going on in my soul, a getting ready for fall that has me more pensive.

All this I thought of while I read the article, which highlighted a book by Gail Sheehy called *Male Passages* and began with a list of signs common to others like me: "Downsizing. Kids leaving home. A friend dropping dead of a heart attack. A woman divorcing and abandoning the husband because she wants to find herself. Any of those can make a man feel out of control and [worry] that he is suddenly disappearing over the hill."[38] Sheehy tells men that the years between thirty-five and fifty-five may be the roughest years of their lives. "Manopause" is the term she uses. One expert quoted in the article suggested that it's a time of slowing down, of becoming aware of limitations.

Perhaps it is no accident that I went out last night, under the night stars, down the driveway to the street running by our house, to pray. I have been, in my praying, more consciously and more easily letting go of my personal ambitions. I feel less of a sense of urgency to accomplish all my goals. But am I really able to trust God with however my future unfolds?

This psalm is helping me. To know that God knows me—and my future: what could be left to worry about? What does God not know?

And of my fears of God's coming too close for comfort? The psalmist knows it well: "You hem me in," he says. That certainly sounds like a limitation, potentially more profound than any of those of mid-life. But to David this intimate involvement did not restrict. It did not stifle. Just as in a sound and rich marriage, the physical and emotional intimacies get only richer, deeper, over the years, so it is true that such closeness requires some restrictions. Some limits. But these are ultimately not limits that cramp us; rather, they allow us to grow. They give us freedom to become more fully ourselves, safe in the security of commitment. To be "hemmed in" means to be held close and safe by God. It means one person will love us and stick by us forever.

Does not such intimate foreknowledge imply inevitability? Futility? Does it not consign us to impersonal fate, to a slow, grinding, impervious divine will? No, the point, rather, is that nothing surprises God. Nothing can blindside him. Because nothing happens that fazes God, I need never fear.

☙

Not long ago I substituted for the regular first-grade Sunday school teacher at church. *I* learned something, as it turned out. I stood before a half-dozen six- and seven-year-olds with verses from Psalm 139 in my hand: "God knows me full well," I read to the classroom full of spruced and squirmy kids. And from a later verse in the psalm: "He knit me together in my mother's womb." But this is not a knowledge to make us afraid, I explained. It should make us happy.

To show what I meant, I had the kids pair off with this assignment: "I want you to count the hairs on each other's heads," I said. At first all I got were embarrassed looks. But Sam and Tom and Lisa and Julia began, giggling as they pulled apart the strands of each other's hair. Other kids got relaxed enough to try, too. Of course, it didn't take long for them to discover they couldn't hope to count every filament, each follicle. That was the point.

"If we had an hour left," I said, "we still couldn't do it."

Then I said, "Let me read you another verse from the Bible, this one from Jesus." And I read Luke 12:7, where Jesus, pointing to God's loving kindness, God's knowing love of us, told his followers, "The very hairs on your head are numbered."

"How carefully God watches out for us, and cares for us," I said. "All the hairs—too many to count—God can see."

I don't know if the message got all the way home. I'm not sure how much the children grasped. But then I thought, *Listen to what you are trying to tell them.*

What more do I need to know?

Persistence

Give me grace, O God, to hear your calling and to follow your guiding. . . . You offer us yourself and all your goods. Give us grace to receive them. You show us the way to irreplaceable benefits; enable us not to turn aside, until we have taken possession of them.

Give us constancy and steadiness of purpose, that our thoughts may not be fleeting, fickle, and ineffectual, but that we may perform all things with an immovable mind to the glory of your holy name. Through Christ our Lord. [39]
—LUDOVICUS (JUAN LUIS) VIVES

I'M GRATEFUL TODAY. AS I GET SHAVED AND dressed, I think of how I have daydreamed for years about the life I live now. *To spend most of my work hours writing about spirituality,* I tell myself . . . *what a godsend!*

I don't always overflow with gratitude, of course—not when deadlines press hard, not when I take daily pleasures for granted. But today I remember how God has seemed to guide me to where I am. How I began to feel a call years ago that has led me here. I felt the call intensely, but still, I would scratch my head in puzzlement. With a thriving family to support, with three growing children, how could I possibly make writing for a living work financially? I once heard at a workshop for aspiring writers that someone tallied the number of Americans who earn their livelihood from their writing. The number was ludicrously low.

And yet one thing after another came together to make something very close to that possible, or at least conceivable, for me. Like when my full-time job in publishing vanished when the company closed shop, leaving me suddenly free to pursue freelancing. Jill took on a job that, while paying a meager salary, nevertheless provided full medical insurance for our family. I have been able to supplement our income with a part-time job that left many of my waking hours free for writing.

Still, doing so has been rife with uncertainty. We face risks. What if we miss paying the mortgage some month? What if I have trouble finding publishers who want my *next* book? More immediately on my mind are cash flow challenges as my oldest child, Abram, heads off for college. How will I pay his first tuition bill? I grow anxious. And I pray, *Give me grace to hear your calling and follow your guiding.*

For the question, I see today, has little to do with the "what ifs" my mind likes to toy with. Rather, it is, *Will I let my fear keep me from doing what is the best, even if riskier, thing?* Far worse, I tell myself, were I to fail to be true to what I believe God is calling me to do.

∽

My friend, John, an old friend from Princeton Seminary days, visiting me from New Zealand, seems to confirm this direction. As I showed him the prayer, penned by a (now) little-known Spanish reformer who lived in the early sixteenth century, John said it reminded him of something a Scottish theologian once said: that nothing grieves the heart of God more than that he has so much to offer, yet we fail to avail ourselves of it. We fail to take what he provides us for our journey. So I pray, with a mentor who preceded me on this earth by centuries, *You offer us yourself and all your goods. Give us grace to receive them.*

God can be trusted, this prayer tells me. We can take the risk of following, and then perhaps running into a wall. Vives, a philosopher, social reformer, and educator knew what it meant to have to hold on by the fingernails of sheer trust. His was no typical sheltered life of the writer of scholarly tomes. He was forced to flee Spain in 1509 because of the Inquisition. His opposition to Henry VIII's divorce from Catherine led to his arrest. But he knew God could help supply conviction and courage he could not muster by himself. *You show us the way to irreplaceable benefits.* I pray, *Lord you make possible what could never be true without your presence.*

∞

The prayer grounds me for the future, as well. *Give us constancy and steadiness of purpose, that our thoughts may not be fleeting, fickle, and ineffectual.* It reminds me of the stamina I will need as I follow God's call on my life. Leadership, my wife heard someone say, requires vision, persistence, and stamina. The same could be said for following God into the risky byroads and along the mysterious paths he may open before us.

We are not helped toward faithful persistence by our temptation to live in a rush. Some things require staying power, pressing on one small step at a time. I need to live out the title of one of Eugene Peterson's books, a line in turn taken from a philosopher: "A long obedience in the same direction." Praying Vives's prayer for a week won't complete the process, but it is a start. So with Juan Luis I ask for help from God, *that I may perform all things with an immovable mind to the glory of your holy name.*

God, "who began a good work in you," as the apostle Paul reminded his contemporaries and generations of believers to follow, "will carry it on to completion until the day of Christ Jesus" (Philippians 1:6). So I will remember not to give up too easily when challenges face me this week, when God's new assignments for me take me in unforeseen directions. Or when my newfound sense of calling to ministry takes more time and energy than I expect.

I want an immovable mind. Not to be hard-headed and stubborn, but to be persistent and undiscouragable. So that nothing will thwart God's good designs for me and for the world he has made and continues to redeem and remake.

Wholehearted Devotion

I choose it all, my God. I do not want to become a saint by halves. I am not afraid of suffering for your sake. What I fear is holding on too tightly to my own will. So I give you every-thing; I want only what is your will for me.

—THÉRÈSE OF LISIEUX (AUTHOR'S RENDERING)

I BELIEVE I DETECT A SUBTLE CHANGE working in me through these pray-ers to whom I've been apprenticing myself. Indeed, a change led me to choose a prayer like Thérèse's in the first place, a prayer that has to do with a more far-reaching commitment.

I'm not quite at the place where what I ask through it comes naturally. I mean, do I really give God *everything,* as the prayer has it? Hardly. But at least I *want* such a quality and depth in my faith. At least I find myself *asking.* I'm caught up in myself far too much, still. But a part of me is becoming more concerned about doing God's will. That streak in me that has to grab what I want and that has to prove something to others is relaxing its grip as I yield more to God. I feel less anxious.] A m E N !!

❧

This week I pray in my room at the guest quarters of the monastery of Saint Meinrad in Indiana. I'm compiling a book on

spiritual retreat centers and I came in part for "field research."
But my motives for coming here, and my hopes, go much deeper.
I want to be yanked out of my immersion in the daily duties. The
tasks of normal life too persistently nag at me. I want less temptation to be distracted in God's presence—at least for a few days.

As I join the monks for their evening worship service, I find
my longing confirmed powerfully in the airy Romanesque
church. We are hearing (sometimes chanting) the "Daily Office,"
following the monks in their patterned interaction with
Scripture. The words we are singing, from Lamentations 2:19,
echo through the arches and lofty rafters:

> Arise, cry out in the night, as the watches of the night begin.
> Pour out your heart like water in the presence of the Lord.

The phrase hovers in the evening air. *What does it mean,* I ask
myself, *to pour out my heart like water?* Surely it involves doing so
freely, without hesitation, letting it all flow away and out. It
means, I think, to want, like Thérèse, the "whole thing," to want
God to preside and reside in everything.

But what did Thérèse mean, in her holy impatience, by
declaring her resolve not to become a saint "by halves"?

Her own story, in the autobiography where she shares this
prayer, gives part of the answer. She draws on a childhood memory to explain. One day, Thérèse recalled, her older sister, Léonie,
brought to Thérèse and her younger sister a basket of dolls'
clothes, ribbons, and other odds and ends. Thérèse surmised that
Léonie had decided she was too old to play with dolls. "Here you
are," she told her sisters is a sweeping gesture of generosity. "Take
what you want." Sister Céline, says Thérèse, took a little bundle
of silk braid.

"I thought a moment," remembers Thérèse, "then stretched out my hand and declared, 'I choose everything,' and, without more ado, I carried off the whole lot." And, she concludes, with perhaps a twinkle in her eye, "Everyone thought this quite fair."

Thérèse saw in the story more than a cute four-year-old's antics. "I think," she reflected, "this trait of my childhood characterizes the whole of my life; and when I began to think seriously of perfection, I knew that to become a Saint, one had to suffer much, always aim at perfection and forget oneself." [40]

Marie Francoise-Thérèse Martin, born in France in 1873, was spiritually precocious even as a young child. She was admitted to a convent just three months after her fifteenth birthday. After an outwardly uneventful life, she died there at the age of twenty-four, racked by harrowing respiratory illness. Her one and only book, from which this prayer comes, written at the tail end of the nineteenth century, became an international publishing phenomenon. French soldiers carried her picture into the trenches and heartaches of World War I, *before* the Catholic Church formally named her a saint in 1925. Leaders hailed her simple little book as a piercing testimony to faith, a classic of devotion. I must admit, as I leaf through it, it exudes a self-mortifying piety I am not used to. But I am drawn to the intensity of her spiritual desire.

☙

A "saint" has never been seen by the church as a perfect person, of course. Indeed, in the New Testament the "saints" refer to all believers, made righteous through Christ's redeeming work alone. But of course, there is that other meaning, as when we say of someone dear and faithful, "She was a true saint." This is what we commonly mean—a saint, as the *Oxford Dictionary of Saints* has it, in the sense of being a "man or woman who gives himself, herself, to God heroically."

To many of us there is something odd, even cloying in the air of piousness that seems to surround many of the best-known saints recognized by the Catholic Church. Many of their biographies ooze a too-sweet spirituality. Their chroniclers gloss over honest struggles. The stories sometimes portray an otherworldly medieval Catholic mysticism foreign to our "just the facts" culture. And we find ourselves suspicious of those who seem to hyperspiritualize and thereby hide their human motives. A life supposedly lived for the sole benefit of others may cover hidden manipulations.

But even so, next to the futility of many of the "successes" I have dreamed about, how much more worthy a goal is sanctity. *Holiness* does not carry a lot of currency as a word for our times, but there is a clean freshness, a compelling attraction in what it actually means. "Give me an undivided heart," I read in a psalm this week, "that I may fear your name" (Psalm 86:11). That is another way to ask not to be a saint by "halves."

♋

In the air-conditioned monastery library, where I escape the heat of a cloudless Indiana June afternoon, a book on spiritual growth catches my eye. "Unfortunately," I read, "most people who are drawn to the spiritual life pursue it half-heartedly or inconsistently. We organize life around the call of God but with an all-too-familiar pattern of distraction and conflicting goals."[41] Too true, sadly, for me. I see too much of myself in that description. I've tried to alleviate that some by getting away for this spiritual retreat. I am praying for at least some of young Thérèse's virtue. I ask myself, *How much is the spiritual life something that I am* merely "into," but that doesn't necessarily engulf and engross me? I want God to be more than a hobby.

A simple French girl whom popes and peasants alike read and revered, reminds me that there are far more significant occupations than the flickering attractions of what I too often consider important. *What I fear is holding on too tightly to my own will,* she prayed. So I ask myself, *What if* that *became my greatest concern?* Not how my work will be received, not how many compliments I get for what I have to offer, not how many CDs and sharp clothes I amass. But that my own will not dominate my life?

Such an overarching goal requires something far greater, of course, than resolutions framed by a few days at a spiritual retreat. It means disciplined effort. It means pursuing whole-heartedly what I understand as God's best when I return home to my normal routine. This pursuit of holiness is not something sought even remotely in halves. It will take all of my heart. All of my best.

May God help me. May God help me even *want* to want his help. If he does, there is hope.

Letting Life Unfold

Teach me to seek you, Lord.
Show me where and how. . . .
Have sympathy with our work and our efforts to find you;
we can do nothing without you.
You have invited us to come, please now help us.

—ANSELM, *PROSLOGION*
(AUTHOR'S RENDERING)

LAST WEEK, ON MY RETREAT, I FOUND Anselm's words in a flourishing, framed calligraphy poster on the monastery wall in Indiana. When I saw it, I knew I had stumbled across this week's prayer. It has hit me with a new force.

The simple prayer acknowledges something I have been neglecting: the place of grace. I have not been letting life unfold gently. Up until my coming, I have been pushing and driving, working long hours, getting things settled on the home front before leaving. The days leading up to my trip have been full of *my* plans and thoughts. And now I find that even here in a monastic climate, on this retreat where I am supposed to seek God for the health of my soul, I'm still charging hard. I am fretting over unfinished projects, racing ahead in my mind to dream up new ones. I carry about with me such a need to be involved with any and everything!

Even in the spiritual life I sometimes turn my approach to God into an outline of duties to accomplish. I don't exactly lapse into the old heresy of Pelagius, the British monk who centuries ago turned Christianity into an arduous struggle for perfection, devoid of a robust sense of God's role in the enterprise. Still, a part of me has not learned to depend enough on God. I constantly want to rush in and get things done. I tend to act before I pray, accomplish before I wait, impatiently tap my fingers on the steering wheel when stuck in traffic when instead I could enjoy a pause in my rush to the next destination.

Anselm is reminding me of a better way. Not that he didn't struggle, too. The eleventh-century monk and philosopher shared this incessant drive to "do," I suspect. Even on his deathbed, a story goes, when you would think he would be worrying only about putting his soul in order to meet his Maker, he was thinking, instead, about a book he felt constrained to write. When his fellow monks told him on Palm Sunday of 1109 that he would surely be in Christ's heavenly presence by Easter, he said he was willing to go. But he would prefer to stay to finish his treatise on a philosophical problem (the origin of the soul). He died with pen in hand, the book unfinished.[42]

Anselm's prayer does reflect a vigorous seeking, of course. It is not about becoming passive. Anselm was no quietist. His was a life of much urgency and passion. He appears in the history books as one of the church's early great thinkers (college students still ponder his "ontological argument" for the existence of God). He was a forerunner (perhaps even founder) of what is called scholastic philosophy. His was a mind ever active.

But he lived and prayed with a calm conviction that Someone works in any situation before he could even think or move. Someone already works in *us*. "Prevenient grace," the Methodists would later call the idea that God draws us to himself even before we care much or even know we need God. Anselm knew that the life of faithfulness acknowledges God as previous and prior. We cannot pride ourselves on our earnestness, but rather humbly ask God to teach us to seek him in the first place. *Teach me to seek you, Lord. Show me where and how.* I see how Anselm learned to still the outward motion and inner commotion, at least at times.

A friend told me recently of how she attended a church that prided itself on spiritual fervor and strong commitment. She had been attracted by the vibrancy, the intensity. But the urgency began to wear her down. She told me, "I'm tired of people calling me to get radical for God. I don't think God would mind if we just rested for a time and let God be radical."

How often are we tempted to think that *we* are the ones who count most, that God is to be called in only to bless our efforts, once we think we've done our best? It is an approach to life summed up in the phrase *God as afterthought.* Or God as supplement. We too often place our emphasis on what we *do,* not on how we pray.

I want a different way, Lord. I want to be done with too much self-reliance. *We can do nothing without you,* I pray.

And then I realize that just my being here in this monastic setting, away from my office for a three-day retreat, acknowledges that grace at work. I am not only stepping back from the push and pull, but inviting a gracious God in. I am creating a space in a busy life for a God I know in my better moments I cannot do without. Some of that sense of God's necessary grace infuses this prayer. *You have invited us to come, please now help us.*

∞

Back home, later in the week, I lay the prayer on the passenger seat as I run errands in the car and let Anselm's words permeate my thoughts. As I look ahead to multiple tasks, I have to confess how antsy and urgent I have been feeling. But once again, the prayer almost immediately brings me peace. It allows me to form words I could not, in my frenetic, near-frantic state, produce out of the thin air of my interior distractedness.

I need not do it all, I am mercifully reminded. *Have sympathy with our work and our efforts to find you,* I learn to say. There is One who remembers me. Even when I, caught in my web of distractions, forget. I can relax and let life unfold . . . gently.

Nothing Matters More than God

I know what I should do.
Only now am I becoming a true follower.
May nothing of forces visible and invisible hold me back,
  that I may attain to Jesus Christ.
Come fire and cross and striving with wild animals,
  the rending of my bones and wrenching of my limbs,
  even the torments of the Evil One,
  Just let me attain to Jesus Christ.
—IGNATIUS OF ANTIOCH (AUTHOR'S RENDERING)

AS ABRAM, MY OLDEST, GETS READY TO
leave for college, he spends days sorting through accumulated years of guitar music, books, outgrown clothes, and Bible quizzing competition trophies. While he packs, he sometimes grows reflective, curious about the adventure ahead. And sometimes anxious.

"Dad," he said to me recently, "I feel like I'm being attacked spiritually. It seems like there are forces trying to disturb me and distract me."

"This is a scary time," I told him. "Leaving home and launching a new stage of life naturally causes you anxious moments." I was right in part, of course. But what I was thinking was, *No need to over-spiritualize.* I too quickly downplayed, even dismissed, the way in which life sometimes does resemble a battle. Our lives are played out within a greater cosmic drama, often unseen, but nevertheless real.

"Are there really forces that dive, invisible," writes one writer on angels, "into our petty affairs?"[43] In my middle-class American life, I enjoy material comfort and religious freedom. I am shielded from most violence and pestilence and repression, and in my amazing technological connectedness to instantaneous information, I forget the realms I may not see. How important, then, to increase my awareness of the struggle for good and evil that wages all around me and within me. How appropriate, as this prayer reminds me, to say, *May nothing of forces visible and invisible hold me back.*

∽

Religious persecution rages in spots across the globe. I have only to go to church on Sunday to know it. My church learned some months ago of a swelling population of Sudanese refugees in Nashville. They have begun coming to our worship services on Sundays, bringing with them a faith tested in a crucible of martyrdom and torture. We hear the stories from their land—of women raped, of men slaughtered, of children enslaved, of villages raided. They know what it means to be persecuted for no reason other than their allegiance to Jesus.

Perhaps all that was behind my choosing this prayer, the original translation of which I found in a collection of prayers of martyrs.[44] This cry is from a man whose Christian faith would lead to his imprisonment and death. So again, as I read and pray it, Ignatius's prayer significantly stretches me, like the one from

Thérèse of Lisieux did two weeks ago. The sentiment behind the ancient words reminds me of the hardship and suffering that loyalty to God sometime entails, in any era.

But something about Ignatius's prayer strikes me as odd right off. *Only now am I becoming a true follower,* he says. This first-century Christian, a bishop of Antioch in Syria, only just *now* becoming a true believer, toward the end of his life? Ignatius was known as faithful and brave, even before his refusal to honor pagan gods and his courageous stand before the Roman emperor that would ultimately send him to execution. Yet when it came to his natural clinging to life, to the bending of his will, he now saw how much he had to learn.

Perhaps Ignatius wanted to imitate Jesus and his death, much like Paul the apostle wanted to do.[45] Perhaps he also feared his own fragile humanity, that his nerve would not hold as he looked ahead to the long journey from Syria to Rome where he would meet his fate. Emperor Trajan himself heard the case against Ignatius, I learn, heard his defense and tersely sentenced him—to death. Ignatius would walk out into an arena to become food for wild animals under the watching eyes of the Roman throngs. Ignatius may have been steeling himself against the pain he knew he would face. So he fortified himself, telling himself, in effect, how he must not turn from the faith to which he had so publicly committed himself.

Some find such embracing of martyrdom macabre, masochistic. Some of the early Christians did perhaps go too far in seeing death in the arena or at the fiery stake as a glorious finale. But the raw testimony of the martyrs will not let me sit too complacently in my daily pleasures and easy demands. They remind me that I don't want to become too composed a person, too comfortable a Christian. They remind me how nothing matters more than God. Nothing.

Ignatius felt that his intimacy with God, growing as it had all his life, would now find a truer expression, and he was willing to suffer even death if it could thereby happen. This prayer I pray this week appeared in one of the many letters he sent to churches as he journeyed toward his death. I see something fiery, gritty, honest about his facing of death. But still, I wonder, would I be similarly faithful?

It is not easy, then, to pray as Ignatius did. But when you confront the worst, he seems to say, *fire and cross and striving with wild animals, the rending of . . . bones and wrenching of . . . limbs, even the torments of the Evil One,* a certain freedom, to be God's own, comes. As well as a singleness of purpose. I am reminded of the nineteenth-century Danish philosopher Kierkegaard's dictum, that "purity of heart is to will one thing."[46] *Lord, may it be so.*

∾

My life contains and conveys much that is pleasant. This morning's run, though warm, was invigorating. As I came up the driveway, I looked at our two-story Cape Cod and with quiet amazement felt a wave of gratitude. *How privileged I am to live here,* I thought. *Thank you, God, for such abundant blessings.*

But none of it allows me to courageously face death. No, for that, I need faith and passion. So I pray,

> *May nothing of forces visible and invisible hold me back,*
> *that I may attain to Jesus Christ.*

When Ignatius heard his sentence from Trajan, an early church historian wrote, he cried out with joy. I'm sure I would cry out with panic or anguish. But within me there is also a recognition of deeper realities. Some things make life, even death, somewhat dwarf in importance.

"I thank you, O Lord," Ignatius prayed when convicted by the Emperor, "that you have entrusted me with a mature love for you; you have made me to be bound with iron chains, like your apostle Paul." And it was no mere show. Early historians tell us, "Having spoken thus, he then, with delight, clasped the chains about him; and when he had first prayed for the church, and commended it with tears to the Lord, he was hurried away by the savage cruelty of the soldiers, like a distinguished ram the leader of a goodly flock, that he might be carried to Rome, there to furnish food to the bloodthirsty beasts."[47]

But neither his life nor his death was lost. Not to God. Not to the church. Not to me, for I need such a mentor to show me how to let a martyr's courage come to live in me!

Heart Afire

*Set our hearts on fire with love to you, O Christ our God,
that in its flame we may love you with all our heart, mind,
soul, and strength and love our neighbors as ourselves, so that,
keeping your commandments, we may glorify you, the giver of
all good gifts.*

—EASTERN ORTHODOX PRAYER
(AUTHOR'S ADAPTATION)

THIS MORNING, I THINK, *IT WOULDN'T
hurt for someone to set my heart ablaze.* I feel sluggish,
dormant, despite the ninety-degree temperatures expected for
this July day.

"Aren't you getting up?" Jill asked as I lay in bed. As a morning person, I normally bound out of bed long before her. But
today's accumulating backlog of tasks is not energizing me, as
deadlines sometimes do, but making me draggy.

Fortunately, as I mentally sorted through the tasks to come
and stretched one last time before rising, I thought of this
prayer. I prayed it then, as I pray it now, sitting at my desk with
the day beginning in earnest. I form the words not as exuber-
antly as I may another day, but faithfully. Ready to make it a
beginning.

And then I think, *how fleeting, even foolish, my worries seem.*

Instead of obsessing and seizing on so many little things, why can't I burn with a love for God and a compassion for others that makes every other fear or concern dwindle and sputter out?

༄

Set our hearts on fire. I say this to a God who, I recall, is often symbolized by fire. Ancient cultures not only revered fire for all the ways it warmed their homes and lit the darkness, but they also worshiped God with fiery altars. Some worshiped fire itself.

I recall, as I pray, how the Bible finds in fire a way to at least begin to depict God's unsearchable, refining radiance. The metaphor helped people realize that God is no tame deity whose power and expectations are easily quenched. The Israelites found that the glory of God "looked like a consuming fire," a "devouring" fire, someone else translates it (Exodus 24:17). A pillar of fire accompanied them on their wilderness journey to the land flowing with milk and honey God had promised. Much later, the disciples, meeting the resurrected Jesus on the Road to Emmaus, not knowing who it was at first, realized his presence when they found their hearts "burning," or, to put it more graphically, "on fire" (Luke 24:32). The presence of Jesus had that kind of effect on them.

༄

Later in the week, as I talk with a friend at work, she tells me a fascinating story about the God of fire. She had attended an Academy of Spiritual Formation, an interdenominational program in spiritual life, and she got to know one of the leaders of the sessions. "I'm praying that you become all fire," the leader said to her after one conversation.

"I didn't understand just what she meant," Mary Lou told me. But she knew enough of the biblical imagery to see how such a prayer might make sense.

After the conference, she told me, she came across a story, one with great relevance for one praying for a heart set on fire. A story I, too, think about as I pray this prayer.

It concerns the fourth-century Christians known as the Desert Fathers and Mothers. These Syrian and Egyptian believers fled what they considered the compromises and watered-down faith of their cities. They went to the deserts of Egypt to pray and seek God. They lived simply, austerely, refusing to let anything distract them from their faith. Sometimes they were joined by followers who wanted to learn more.

Once Abba Joseph, the story goes, was approached by one of his students. "I pray some," he said, "I sing some psalms, I fast. As far as lies in my power, I cleanse my thoughts. Now what more should I do?"

The old teacher stood up and spread out his hands and his fingers, resembling lamps of fire. "Why not," he said, "become totally fire?"[48]

Why not, I tell myself, *burn with fiery passion for God? Why not become consumed by it?*

֍

This will mean concrete changes for me, I can tell. Fire makes for more than an inner experience. It spreads to others. It can be no accident that tongues as "of fire" appeared at Pentecost when Jesus' first followers gathered to wait for direction. Fire ignited them for their mission, galvanized them with urgency to proclaim the Good News.

So I understand now why I pray not only for a heart on fire, but *that in its flame we may love you with all our heart, mind, soul, and strength and love our neighbors as ourselves.* These phrases send me back to Jesus' articulation of the two greatest commandments. A teacher of the Jewish Law had come up to Jesus and asked, "Of all the commandments, which is the most important?"

"The most important one," answered Jesus, "is this: 'Hear, O Israel, the Lord our God, the Lord is one. Love the Lord your God with all your heart and with all your soul and with all your mind and with all your strength.' The second is this: 'Love your neighbor as yourself.' There is no commandment greater than these."

The teacher was impressed and, adding his own agreement, said, "To love [God] with all your heart, with all your understanding and with all your strength, and to love your neighbor as yourself is more important than all burnt offerings and sacrifices" (Mark 12:28–31, 33).

To love God with my whole being, and, irresistibly, to love my neighbor as myself, to love those I come into contact with today—here in my own house, at the office, with people I phone! How can I do it? I get so caught up in the stifling worries and anxieties that beset me. I need to be taken out of myself.

In another coincidence (divine reinforcement?) I find an article in *US News & World Report* entitled, "What Came Before Creation?" It tells of the swirling abundance of new theories of the universe's origins. I read this line: "The earliest big-bang theories held that if all matter had once been pressed into a pinpoint, it must have also been incomprehensibly hot, because compression generates heat."[49] Then came, many scientists believe, the explosion that sent the universe's matter spinning into space's outer reaches—the big *bang*.

The science of that picture is open to question, of course, to say nothing of sorting out how such a theory relates to *God's* having created the universe. But I find myself struck by a larger point. The physical matter of the universe is not made to contract. The chemical reaction of oxygen, heat, and fuel drives outward explosively. Fire will not be contained.

When *my heart is set aflame, O God,* I cannot stay content pulled into myself. With a heart and soul and mind and strength ablaze with love for God, something combusts. Love launches me Godward. My faith drives me into a wider world, into the lives of others.

And so I pray, *How faintly do I love you, O Lord! How much do I need your Holy Spirit's fire!* How cool my soul's embers, my concern for others.

But here I am, Lord, praying for a different way. Praying to become fire. Totally fire.

Inclusive Intercession

We bring to you, O Lord, the troubles and dangers of people and countries, the cries of prisoners and the captured, the griefs of the bereaved, the needs of strangers, the powerlessness of the weak, the sadness of the bone tired, and the declining abilities of the elderly. O Lord, draw near to each; for the sake of our Lord Jesus Christ.

—ATTRIBUTED TO ANSELM, ADAPTED

AT MY SUNDAY SCHOOL CLASS I JUST taught that we can pray with a newspaper in hand. And come to our paper or news broadcasts with prayers in our hearts. I have been teaching a half-dozen eager learners, some of whom pray more faithfully than I do, I suspect. But I have some ideas for them. "Ways to revitalize your devotional times," is my angle.

Stories of children orphaned by an accident, a cancer patient battling for life, a company victimizing and exploiting workers, all belong in our prayers, I said. God wants us not only to care, but to *pray.* I mentioned that bombings, starving children, scandals in high places, spiritually lost leaders, and warring nations remind us how, in the apostle Paul's words, "the whole creation has been groaning as in the pains of childbirth right up to the present time" (Romans 8:22).[50]

Last week's prayer, with its fiery conviction and compassion, helped open me to the needs of a wider world. This week's prayer, phrportedly penned by the eleventh-century theologian and church leader very much in touch with daily realities, helps me practice what I encourage my class to do: fill prayer with the everyday grist and grit of life. Such a prayer, such an approach to God, was a gift of this archbishop of the medieval English church. He used (in the original language) rhymed prose and bold images. Unlike so many of his colleagues in church leadership, Anselm wrote for laypeople as well as for monks. He didn't assume that prayer always had to be liturgical and prescribed. His prayers, both subtle and theologically daring, opened wide doors for individual praying. Just what I need. Just what my students seem to need.

And how it helps to use Anselm's intercessory categories as a frame or scaffolding to give breadth and definition to our too-often random thoughts.

෨

We bring to you, O Lord, the troubles and dangers of people and countries. . . .

The news today reported that the death toll from storms in Papua New Guinea exceeds 1,200, with thousands still missing. I inwardly shudder at the images of bodies pulled from the water so badly decomposed that they fall apart. The decaying flesh will harbor disease, the newscaster said, which workers fear will spread quickly among the storm-weakened survivors. *Such a world we live in, O Lord! Be present to the people of this sorrowing, devastated country.*

෨

The cries of prisoners and the captured . . .

I thought of the mass of humanity jailed, and especially those

I once met inside a prison. This is how my well-to-do suburban world interfaced with those locked out of sight and usually out of mind: I had been visiting residents of an apartment complex, telling them about the new church I was pastoring. I happened to knock on the door of a woman prison chaplain. She was large, her speech layered with African American dialect, and her soul fiery for God. When she learned I was a pastor, she invited me along to meet her young incarcerated protégés. She went to the prison at least weekly, teaching the Bible, supporting the inmates, talking straight to them.

To get in to the massive structure on the outskirts of Huntsville, Texas, we passed through a towering fence studded with coils of rolled barb wire. We entered multiple doors, operated by uniformed guards. When we finally got to the prisoners, they overflowed with eagerness for company. Theirs was a dismal life, though the faith that had taken root in the young men we met still quietly amazes me.

And now, thinking of them again, I pray, *Be with these men, O Lord. Be with all the prisoners. Be with those who have lost so much freedom, and often wander through their years of captivity with no hope.*

◦◦

The griefs of the bereaved, the needs of strangers, the powerlessness of the weak, the sadness of the bone tired, the declining abilities of the elderly.

I think of Manier West, who, along with his wife, Edna, have been active in our church for years. Edna just died of cancer. She had fought long and hard and prayerfully, believing she would experience healing, not just through the chemotherapy and radiation, but through those of us she called her "prayer warriors." It was not to be so. But her faith sustained her in profound ways just the same. I think of Manier, who, like another of the categories in the prayer, faces *declining abilities of the elderly.*

And I pray for homeless people, for my mother-in-law, who, God willing, I will see in a few weeks when I take my son to college not far from where she lives.

These are the needs I can bring to prayer. It is the least I can do. Frequently the best.

Anselm's prayer has helped me gather and include and remember. A form like this can stifle, of course, but it can also jog our remembrance of people we love or situations we cannot see or help first-hand. It can order and bring life to what otherwise might be random flashes of prayerful sentiment. It can free the heart's hurts and transmute them into energy for banging on God's door. And so, this week, as I remember these people and situations and many others, I ask, *O Lord, draw near to each, for the sake of our Lord Jesus Christ.*

And I call to mind just how vital intercessory prayer seems to be in the scheme of things. Sometimes I assume that *my* work is what counts most, gets the most "done." But in such times I forget exactly what prayer is, what it effects, who it enlists in the world's crises and my everyday acquaintances' sorrows. The words for prayer in the original languages of the Bible literally mean "ask," "request," even "beg" and "beseech." And no wonder. Asking God to intervene is no futile shouting into a howling winter wind that swallows the sound into nothingness. It gets heard. Not always answered in ways I want or expect. But heard. Embraced by a loving Savior.

I do not pray enough. Not when I think of the world's vast needs. Not when I consider Christ's constant promises in Scripture to listen when we ask, seek, knock.

"Sometimes, when I read a newspaper," one of the students in my Sunday school class told me this week, "I get so depressed I want to throw it down. So much terrible stuff happens." Mary Lee is a white-haired sixty-something woman whose prayers are as passionate and genuine as those of anyone I know. Still, the condition of the world worries her. The thought of turning an exercise in hand-wringing frustration into hand-folding trust in a gracious, active God, *that* would make a difference. "Now I know what to do when I hear such awful stuff," she exclaimed with a jolt of discovery.

She will pray. So will I, when I can remember. When Anselm's gracious, lovely, heart-expanding prayer helps me call to mind at least some of the world's vast need.

A God to Hide In

You are my hiding place;
you will protect me from trouble
and surround me with songs of deliverance.

∽

I will instruct you and teach you [says the Lord]
  in the way you should go;
I will counsel you and watch over you.
Do not be like the horse or the mule,
  which have no understanding
  but must be controlled by bit and bridle
  or they will not come to you.
Many are the woes of the wicked,
  but the LORD's unfailing love
  surrounds the [one] who trusts in him.
Rejoice in the LORD and be glad, you righteous;
  sing, all you who are upright in heart!
                              —DAVID, THE PSALMIST

MY PRAYER THIS WEEK FROM PSALM 32:7–11,
words both addressed to God and words the psalmist hears
as God's reply, came to me through the suggestion of my friend,

Mary Lee. She could tell by the edge in my voice when we talked at church Sunday that I needed reassurance. She knew some of what I was facing. She realized how I needed to be steered to a promise I could stand on.

For, I told her, I would soon work my last day at my part-time job at The Upper Room. I was relieved that my project there was nearing completion, I said. In many ways the day represented a milestone, a fulfillment of a dream to devote myself full time to a ministry of nurturing prayer and writing. I believe it to be a God-given dream. While I still share much responsibility on the home front, I can now focus on what God seems to have led me to in my vocation. But given how much I have looked forward to this day, now that it is upon me I'm surprised at how anxious I feel. How my mind floods with uncertainties!

Just yesterday Jill admitted to mixed feelings about my stopping my part-time work. "I understand your desire to devote yourself to your writing," she said, "and I know we have talked all this through, but the loss of steady income still unsettles me a bit." I realized it did me, too. But that's not all. I am looking even further ahead than the next book project that will earn income for my family. What about this nagging sense that I should pursue ordination in the Episcopal Church? I know from earlier years of full-time pastoring that ministry requires unprecedented stamina and persistence. It is no quick and easy matter to pursue ordination in my denomination, especially. But the call to return to more pastoral, priestly work will not go away.

Mary Lee heard all that questioning and turmoil beneath whatever words I said on Sunday. "I've been praying for you," she told me on the phone this morning. "And I'm especially praying the words spoken by God through the psalm, 'I will instruct you and teach you in the way you should go.'" She wanted to plant her requests to God on my behalf in that divine promise. And now I realize I have my prayer for this week. Now I realize how I need to turn to him for what it will take to keep me moving into tomorrow with trust.

God certainly seems to be trying to get through to me. Also this Sunday, the prayer printed in the church bulletin that our minister prayed aloud, addressed God as "protector of all who trust in you." It went on to ask "that, with you as our ruler and guide, we may so pass through things temporal, that we lose not the things eternal."[51] The language is flowery and old, but beautiful. And certainly to the point.

God is my hiding place, the psalm reminds me this morning as I stare it down, peer into it for every ounce of comfort I can gain. God will become a place where I can duck the onslaughts of my anxieties. Where I can find rest for my continuing rehearsals of worst-case scenarios. Where I can find refuge from my propensity to borrow worries from tomorrow's uncertainties.

Teresa of Avila writes,

> Briefly, in this storm, there is no help for us but to wait upon the mercy of God, who suddenly, at the most unlooked-for hour, with a single word, or some chance occasion, lifts the whole of this burden from the soul, so that it seems as if it has never been clouded over, but is full of sunshine and far happier than it was before. Then, like one who has escaped from a perilous battle and gained the victory, the soul keeps praising our Lord, for it is he who has fought and enabled it to conquer. It knows very well that it did not itself do the fighting.[52]

Teresa's wise words remind me that I don't need to fight all my future's battles now, nor by myself. Why not leave them alone and hide in God, secure in his care?

Of course, this is not a lesson instantly learned. I get dense again and forgetful, so I need to hear the admonishment of the psalm:

> *Do not be like the horse or the mule,*
> *which have no understanding*
> *but must be controlled by bit and bridle*
> *or they will not come to you.*

I want to run to God, not just in the hardships and harrowing moments, but also in the long straight stretches. I want to be led and surrounded. I want something other than agitation when I go through times when things happen more slowly than I expect. When I get anxious for change, almost for its own sake.

> *[B]ut the LORD's unfailing love*
> *surrounds the [one] who trusts in him.*

Like the worshiping throngs depicted in this psalm, in these words taken from Temple worship millennia ago, I find myself aware of One who holds me and holds my future. I will take badly needed refuge in him. At least, today, I will try.

A Vile Worm Am I?

O Lord, you represent everything good. So who am I that I dare to talk to you? I am your poorest and most minor servant, a vile worm, much more poor and worthy of despising than I have courage to say. You know I am nothing—need I remind you?—I have nothing, and I can do nothing. But you—that is a different matter! Only you are good, without fault, and holy. You can accomplish everything, you give all things, you fill to the brim everything. Only the wretched sinner do you leave with hands empty of heavenly joys.

Please, then, remember your kind mercies and fill my heart with your grace. . . . How else can I bear the hardships and stresses unless you bring mercy and grace? Do not turn your face from me. Do not be slow in coming. Do not hold back your comfort, or my soul will become arid like the desert.[53]

—Thomas à Kempis

I HAVE MIXED FEELINGS ABOUT THIS PRAYER, coming across it in my copy of *The Imitation of Christ,* a dog-eared, underlined paperback that I have not revisited in a significant way for years. I first read the book when discovering the Christian classics of devotion, while a very green pastor at my first church after seminary. I found myself awed by the ancient text. It helped me get my focus off of *me,* and at least in moments, call to mind whom I was serving.

Some years later, however, I went to someone for spiritual counsel, and when I mentioned my attraction to *The Imitation of Christ,* he barely concealed a mild disdain for its "otherworldly" tendencies, its "beating myself up" tone. I have tended to look at the book more askance since then.

But this prayer strikes home today. It makes me reflective. I don't find myself growing overly introspective through it; far too much is happening this week for me to have time for that. But it reminds me of the littleness of the concerns that sometimes seem so huge to me. It asks me to stand back from the things swirling by and around me, and bow inwardly before One greater. Something in me cries out for that, though it means facing my weaknesses.

And so I pray it, still not without some mixed feelings, but the words, for all their austerity, do not press me down. No, paradoxically, I try them out believing they hold out hope from new quarters. *How I need that, O Lord.*

⁊

Now that I am deep into the prayer, I realize keenly that its tone pushes against the sentiment of our times. Through much of my life I have heard the cultural motto that whispers (or blasts from ads) that we should live to do little more than pamper ourselves, indulge ourselves, "love" ourselves. Perhaps the "vile worm" language is a bit much. But is shallow self-adulation any better? In our day when high self-esteem is the ultimate god, this prayer reminds me of the virtue of humility. Of the limits of self-esteem.

A parody on the TV program "Saturday Night Live" comes to mind; a parody indeed, but not too far from cultural reality. Pop psychologist Stuart Smalley intoned, chipper but clearly insecure, "I'm *good* enough, I'm *smart* enough, and doggone it, people *like* me." He said it so emphatically that you felt he had yet to talk himself into believing it.

I realize as I pray à Kempis's prayer that there is a reason for the parody. Sometimes I *need* to feel small in the presence of Someone unfathomably large. It is a joke (and not a particularly funny one) to imagine I don't. I appropriately feel shame in the presence of a Love that is incomprehensibly holy. Who am I, after all? A healthy awe of the Most High will not hurt the wholesomeness of my human soul.

The excesses on this side also easily fall into humor, however. I think of my late father-in-law who, with a twinkle in his eye, would sometimes, while puttering around the house or crafting something in his basement wood shop, sing-song a lilting ditty:

> Nobody loves me.
> Everybody hates me.
> Guess I'll go eat worms.

We knew he was kidding, and his song helped him make light, I suspect, of any temptation to wallow in self-pity.

But the excesses are usually *not* funny. I think of the soul-sick, heart-weary person who feels he or she can never be forgiven, convinced he or she will irretrievably face the fate of the damned. Or I think of the times when regret for missteps of my own haunt me; I don't worry that they are unforgivable, but that does not mean I never think about them.

Guilt-mongering, however, does not strike me as the way of life-giving prayer. It is true that the group of devoted monks, for which Thomas apparently served as scribe for the book we now know as *The Imitation of Christ*, took a rigorous approach. His Dutch community was part of a larger movement known as the Brethren of the Common Life. They emphasized self-denial. My friend William Griffin, a Latin scholar and fellow writer, describes them this way: They "stressed things like the humanity of Christ, method in meditation, knowledge of self and fulfillment of obligations, the practice of virtue and the avoidance of vice, retirement from the world, devotional reading of the Scriptures, and a prickly restlessness with intellectuality for its own sake. Because of their enthusiasm for the movement, the Brethren quickly became known as the 'Devouts.'"[54]

So how do I pray this prayer's severe words? Should I really say with à Kempis and his fellow monks, "I am your poorest and most minor servant, a vile worm, much more poor and worthy of despising than I have courage to say. You know I am nothing . . ."? William Griffin captures the starkness even more vividly in his translation: "I'm just Your average pauperous, verminous servant. Much more poor and contemptible than I dare to say and You seem to know."[55] Am I really that low in God's eyes?

I have never been attracted to the God sometimes caricatured as explosively angry or vindictive. I see evidence of God's judgment and wrath in the Bible, of course. I don't want to ignore the reality of God's displeasure at sin. But I think what the monk realizes is not so much about how God hates sin as that next to an inexhaustibly good God, even the best person's best pales. He is, as à Kempis says, *nothing* when placed next to that, if only by comparison. That is not so much to demean who and what he is as much as to magnify all God is. It is a statement as much of comparison as of abject description.

Which points to its great hope. And mine.

Please, then, remember your kind mercies and fill my heart with your grace. . . . How else can I bear the hardships and stresses unless you bring mercy and grace? Do not turn your face from me. Do not be slow in coming. Do not hold back your comfort, or my soul will become arid like the desert.

༄

Over the prayer hangs the shadow of life without God, of course. I cannot escape that. But I also see and want to seize the radiant promise of a God who showers mercy on the penitent. I now believe that the only healthy way for me to confront my sinfulness (which I must do without flinching) is in a climate of grace. Perhaps when God seems distant is not the best time to scrutinize myself. But when I know, or at least nourish hopes, about who God is, I can come clean in inventorying myself. I can admit what I have missed. For when I can recall the Bible's promises of grace, there is hope. I can look long and hard at myself. And then not despair.

༄

In many ways, this prayer comes as a counterpoint to my external, everyday details. I am enjoying a happy time in my life. Soon Abram, like many of his fellow incoming students at Wheaton College, will leave for a wilderness experience the college hosts for freshmen, just before the fall term begins. It pits them—with few tools of civilization—against the ruggedness of dense forest and craggy mountain face. It is grueling, even scary. It teaches self-reliance and encourages spiritual reflection. I feel an air of anticipation in the household. I know I will miss my son, but this is a happy transition.

Tonight we had some of Abram's student and church friends and adult mentors over to our house for a dessert and send-off. They had a chance to ask him details about what he would be doing, if he was looking forward to trekking off to college. And we had a time for those who wished to pray for him out loud. We didn't want him braving life on his own without that kind of support.

Sitting on the sofa in the living room with all the people around us, I thought, *This is the life! I have so much to be grateful for, Lord.* I gazed at my son, ready to launch a new life. *You are indeed kind in mercy.* I also know nothing will hold Abram safe, save God. *Do not hold back your comfort, or my soul will become arid like the desert.* I pray it for me, but also for him. I know the temptations in the big wide world are too pervasive, the stretches of wilderness too wild and real, to be glib about letting him go.

⟳

It is later in the week. I think about what may be my own future transitions. Jill and I just met with a minister who explained more about the ordination process to us. Driving home, I felt a bit overwhelmed by all that lies before us. Richard also showed me a job description for a position he is urging me to apply for—executive director of an international organization devoted to nurturing prayer, the Anglican Fellowship of Prayer. Though I could get excited about devoting full-time hours to prayer, the job looks very demanding. *Which is the right way to go?* I realize I must ask the question, but must also ask it of God. *Lord, I need guidance.*

I also sense that much of the change stretching before me simply comes down to obedience. Now, in my young forties, I have traded in my earlier exuberance for work with a more mature realization that I live by grace. *I am nothing,* I tell God. Not meaning that I don't matter, not meaning that he has not given me gifts. But that next to what he offers, next to the riches he could bring, next to the unseen ways he wants to use me, why cling to my peculiar little ways, my puny accomplishments, my sins, large and small?

That must be part of what à Kempis had in mind when he pondered the state of his soul. By pondering his depravity he found his heart not sad-sack and despairing, but all the more grateful. For the exercise reminded him of a far vaster mercy. After all, I tell myself, he did not let his compunction drive him away. He kept coming back. And always he found grace. Always. As will I.

The Blessing of Restlessness

Our good Lord showed that it is God's great pleasure that a soul come to God naked, plainly, and humbly. For this is the natural yearning of the soul [through] the touching of the Holy Spirit. . . .

God, of your goodness, grant me your self, for you are enough for me, and nothing less that I might ask would be worthy of you. And if I ask for anything less, I still want more. But only in you do I have all.[56]

—JULIAN OF NORWICH

I OFTEN FEEL RESTLESS, IT SEEMS. I MUST BE prone to it. This week I feel it keenly. I sent off my application letter for the prayer fellowship position and have yet to receive word back. I am having trouble concentrating on my writing, all the more difficult when my mind wanders to the impending deadline. Today I feel frustrated at the seeming slowness of time's passage. I want things to *happen.*

I remind myself that times of restlessness are part of life. In one sense I am simply to accept them. But I see another decision. I can see in them a distraction . . . or an invitation. For they can draw me to prayer. The sense that something inside is missing drives me to keep looking out, up. It urges me not to settle for a job or relationship as some kind of Ultimate. Not to expect anything in this world to fully satisfy. Restlessness brings with it the realization that nothing here truly suffices. Which leaves me in a frame of mind to ask what *does*.

∽

Ultimately, restlessness points me to the Ultimate. I see that clearly today. *God of your goodness, grant me your self, for you are enough for me and nothing less that I might ask would be worthy of you.* "We are built," explains Ronald Rolheiser, "in such a manner and touched by God in such a way that we are incurably sick in an advantageous way. This advantageous sickness, restlessness, is felt as longing, urgent longing, which relentlessly draws us towards goodness, beauty, truth, and union. . . . In biblical language, our urgent longings draw us towards seeing face to face."[57]

Julian of Norwich found this to be true, I realize. The fourteenth century, during which this English woman wrote, could drive anyone to fear or restlessness. She witnessed a deeply troubled time in European history. England locked in combat with France in what would be known as the One Hundred Years War. Within the country, King and barons struggled for power. Bubonic plague—the Black Death—hit England when Julian was but a girl. Between a third to a half of the English population died within two years.

For all the trauma and hardship, not surprisingly spiritual life flourished—all through England. As it did for Julian. Likely a conventional nun at first, she eventually confined herself to a cell in a church (St. Julian's in Norwich, named for a male saint, from which she seems to have taken her name). There, as an anchoress (a kind of hermit), she prayed and sought God. And reflected on what she believed were visions from God. One of them forms the basis for this prayer:

And then he showed [me] a little thing, the size of a hazelnut, lying in the palm of my hand, as it seemed to me. It was round as a ball. I looked at it with the eye of my understanding and thought, *What can this be?* It was answered . . . "It is all that is made." I marveled that it could last, for it was so little that it could suddenly have become nothing. I was answered in my understanding, "It lasts and [always will because] God loves it." And so everything has being by the love of God." [58]

∾

So Julian, holed away in her cell, put her conviction about God to the ultimate test. Stripped of family and most conventional comforts, she had little to do but face God. Little to concern herself with but prayer. She was free to try to understand God, free to praise him.

And she found, as English preacher George Whitefield would put it three centuries later when he preached on Christ's invitation to the weary and heavy laden, "Here is mercy upon mercy."[59] Here is what matters. Here is where restlessness finds rest. *If I ask for anything less,* Julian prayed, *I still want more.* I see that in my own restlessness. *But only in you do I have all.*

∾

Another morning, as I pray Julian's prayer, I realize that I have ached with restlessness largely because I sometimes lack the certitude that I am loved. Profoundly and deeply. I don't always *know* that God's love is my ultimate essential. *If only I would let you convince me down in the depths of my being, O God!*

I'm not there. Not yet. Not fully. But when I waver and get restive, I will try to think of a quiet fourteenth-century English woman, hidden from public view, a woman so intent on prayer that she made friends with a lonely, tiny room. And then and there, I will remember, she met God, the One she named the Maker and Keeper and Lover of all that is. The One who holds in his palm—gently—the vast world.

Which means God holds even me. Safe.

God Is Not Nearsighted

Be thou my vision, O Lord of my heart,
Naught be all else to me, save that thou art,
Thou my best thought, by day or by night,
Waking or sleeping, thy presence my light.
                                        —IRISH HYMN

 THIS WEEK'S PRAYER LED TO AN INCIDENT that made me laugh. And then grow quietly amazed.

In my search for a prayer, I had felt a nudge to turn to the great hymns of the faith. As I looked through a book of hymn texts, this one caught my eye, not only because of its perspective, but because it brought back memories. At the Presbyterian seminary I attended in the late seventies, students and faculty alike gathered in Miller Chapel for worship several mornings a week. And we would sing this hymn frequently. Its lilting Irish tune, along with the words crying out for a vision from God, never failed to stir something in me.

So I began this week, not singing the words this time around, but letting them turn me to God. Letting them better orient me. Thomas Merton's prayer about not knowing where he was going launched me into this year of praying with spiritual mentors; again I face a juncture where I can see what lies around the bend only faintly. Where will my interest in ordination go? What should I make of the interest expressed by the search committee for the prayer fellowship position? What of my wife's own interest in returning to school full time this fall to finally finish her Master of Divinity degree? And what about my own struggle to pray in a too-often too-busy life? I do not know. . . .

So I pray to One whose presence, this verse of hymn reminds me, brings light when things are hard to see. Who draws alongside when the next stretch of road looks blurry. One who sees all—and sees for me—when I cannot. My soul suffers from nearsightedness, every bit as real as that in my physical eyes; but I need not despair. Not when Another sees perfectly.

But then the laugh, which quickly became awe. That came today, with me several days into praying this hymn.

Abram left days ago to join his fellow college freshmen in the wilds. He would backpack on steep, rocky trails in Wisconsin, canoe the Northwoods rivers of Michigan's Upper Peninsula, and at one point, spend three days utterly alone to fast. He had all that to look forward to.

But not what happened on his second day. Here is how Abram described it, in a letter we opened as soon as the mail delivered it to our mailbox:

> I really need your prayers. Yesterday was nothing short of miserable. Actually the day was going fine until we started canoeing in the afternoon. We were practicing how to jump out of the canoe if it capsizes. When my partner and I jumped out, I lost my glasses in the water. I guess the force of the water just ripped them off my face. Of course they didn't float.

Minor detail? Not at all. I can still see, but not nearly as well as I should to be doing wilderness stuff. I told both my leaders, who sympathized with me and acknowledged that I am now somewhat disadvantaged.

All this I read with a sinking feeling. But I kept on. And then laughed. What providence!

But you know the amazing thing about it? God is using this to force me to depend on him. I must turn to him for my very ability to see. Like that old hymn, "Be Thou My Vision," I had prayed that God would reveal himself to me like never before, and he hasn't wasted any time. The time here is about my minute by minute, day by day, asking God for help. Because I am weak.

Jill and I made a not-so-comic picture of anxious parents, concerned about our son's foggy eyesight, hundreds of miles away in an inhospitable environment. There were safety issues, of course. How would he do emotionally? We hurriedly called his optometrist to get his prescription. We bought him some glasses, trying to fit them on someone not here, and mailed them immediately. Still, Abram would spend most of his camping experience severely myopic.

But I realized with awe how God was communicating assurance to both my son and me. How could I not feel reverence at this instance of Providence? I let the message of the letter sink in: How wonderfully, clearly God sees. I let the hymn remind me: *Waking or sleeping, thy presence my light.*

I prayed it for Abram, along with Abram. *Despite what I cannot see, O God, you will draw near. You precede me wherever I go.* I grow anxious at what I cannot foresee, finite human that I am, but I need not flail my arms frantically. I catch glimpses filled not with sharply defined details, but rather (and better) a constant, substantial presence of all-knowing Love.

Why worry about what I cannot see clearly when God has perfect vision?

The Rhythms of Praise

You are great, O Lord, and wonderfully to be praised.
Great is your power, and your wisdom cannot be measured.
Humankind, a tiny part of your creation,
  wants to praise you.
People live with continual reminders of their mortality,
  and with living proof that you stand against the proud.
Still, they want to praise you, this humankind that makes up
  a tiny part of your creation.
You move us to want to praise you.
For you made us for yourself,
And our hearts are restless until they find rest in you.
          —AUGUSTINE (AUTHOR'S RENDERING)

JILL CAME HOME FROM THE OFFICE TODAY with a photocopy of this prayer from Augustine's *Confessions*, taped onto a heart-shaped slip of paper torn from her memo pad. She had run across it thumbing through a book on nurturing faith in children. I had read it before, prayed it before. But as with so much of Augustine's writing, I knew there were riches yet to mine.

I asked Jill what prompted her to copy it for me.

"I thought you probably didn't have many prayers of praise for your book."

Ah, she knows me too well.

Few prayers *are* as focused on praise to God as this one. Or quoted as often, especially the line about our hearts staying restless until they "find rest in you."

With so much positioning itself for my attention now, with my mind tending toward very earthly compulsions, what prayer could better keep my eyes on what matters most? I fall into its rhythms of appreciative words for another realm.

᠙

Much has happened in the last few days, since Jill first brought the prayer to me. Early today we left for Abram's college, driving eleven hours in a minivan crammed with his belongings—clothes, a bike, three guitars, and, of course, his brother and sister. His wilderness camp experience over, classes and orientation about to begin, we came to move him out of our home and into his dorm.

Things were hectic last night as we wedged everything in our Chrysler, making sure we had all the boxes Abram had packed before leaving for his trip. This morning we took back roads that the map suggested as shortcuts. But they ended up slowing us terribly, adding stress when we realized we would show up late at our hosts' home. But there Abram was, in the parking lot of the dorm, tanned, eager, a bit nervous about the year's impinging changes. And this evening we have visited with our hosts, the Millers, old friends from when we lived in the Wheaton area. Tomorrow we get up early to attend parents' orientation. But every now and then in the midst of the bustle I've pulled out my heart-shaped slip with Augustine's prayer taped on it.

> *You are great, O Lord, and wonderfully to be praised.*
> *Great is your power, and your wisdom cannot be measured.*

Even scanning it at odd moments is helping me to remember God, to pull awareness back to the heart of things—the core of all I have been about but take for granted in the blur of activity. I don't want to forget to praise One who made and knows all that I see and experience.

⌘

There was more to the trip. While still in Illinois, we visited Jill's mother. With her Parkinson's Disease, she requires a nursing home's care.

As we entered her hospital-like room, Mom Zook greeted us warmly and seemed alert and optimistic, if almost completely blind. We wheeled her out under the shade of an August early afternoon and spread on the picnic table the take-out pizza we had brought. The wooded grounds of St. Joseph's Home for the Aged, a former convent and school for orphaned children, reminded us of the Creator's hand.

But there was something unsettling about the visit, too. Not just seeing Jill's mother's increasing infirmity and immobility. Among her fellow residents I saw bodies in disarray—unfocusing eyes, jabbering voices, twitching limbs. I saw frames bent and bound to wheelchairs by legs that no longer worked. I passed one woman in the hallway exuding the acrid smell of urine, eyes hungry for human contact. Another older woman clutched a doll, her "baby." Some were fighting boredom and lack of human contact. Some had just resigned themselves to it.

With Mom back in her bed, we saw someone just outside the door push an ambulance stretcher up the hallway. Before long the ambulance attendants brought the stretcher back the way they had entered—with a body shrouded in a bag. Another resident had died—the third within just days, Mom told us somberly. I was sobered, of course.

Back at our hotel, waiting to check ourselves in, I pulled out Augustine's prayer once again. Even here, amid broken bodies, perhaps especially here, I realized, we can and must live with praise on our lips. Later the prayer would move me even more when I discovered that a portion was left out of what Jill copied for me:

> *People live with continual reminders of their mortality,*
> *and with living proof that you stand against the proud.*
> *Still, they want to praise you . . .*

༾

We're back home, tired from the trip. I miss Abram already, and I know I have hard work left on my writing project. I tend to give too much weight to my feelings, I know. So I found it easy to forget to praise God. But my prayer reminds me that doing so is more than a pleasant diversion. Praise is basic to the rhythms of creation, the rhythms of my heart.

You move us to want to praise you. It is for wherever I am, whatever I'm doing. *For you made us for yourself.* Praise is what I am made to do. *And our hearts are restless until they find rest in you.*

Sending Worries Prayerward

Give ear to my words, O LORD,
  Consider my sighing.
Listen to my cry for help,
  My King and my God,
For to you I pray.
In the morning, O LORD, you hear my voice;
  In the morning I lay my requests before you
  And wait in expectation.

—DAVID, THE PSALMIST

WHAT A WEEK. TOO MUCH COMING TOO fast: I awaken weighed down by all the tasks to be done: a retreat to plan and lead, three of my books in various stages of publication, then a meeting to prepare for with the group charged to confirm (or question) my call to ordination. All of these come with their own demands, timetables, stresses. The urgencies press in hard. I feel not just busy, but pulled apart, distracted. I can identify with the psalmist's talk of "sighing" in this prayer in Psalm 5:1–3.

So this morning I awake early, thinking not only about my restless anxiety, but also my need for prayer. I feel great motivation to get up, sit in the living room, light a candle (to set this apart as a prayer time, even when my mind wanders), and invite

God in. I repeat a simple phrase, *Lord, here I am.* I thank God for the day. And I ask for help. *Consider my sighing, O Lord.*

Even as I'm asking, my mind turns to verse 3 of David's prayer. What it describes becomes reality for me, even as I ask:

> *In the morning I lay my requests before you*
> *And wait in expectation.*

How simple, I think. Why can't I learn more quickly to send my worries prayerward instead of holding them tightly? I feel hope again that the responsibilities and activities and duties won't swamp me, inundating my waking hours. Rather, they will take their proper place. God can tame the roar of their demands, their pushiness. I can stop sighing inwardly.

〰

I must be a slow learner. It's another day, and yesterday's insight did not carry me long. Out running this morning, I took along these scripture verses and a card jotted with the names of people and situations I pray for. I started on the list as I lifted leaden legs. The whole enterprise seemed heavy, forced. But then I read, "You hear my voice." I think, *What a promise!* I stop running for a minute, slowing to a walk, and I think, *What could matter more? Surely this corresponds with the reality of the situation more than anything I can devise to add to my worry list.*

For some reason a brief saying of Andrew Murray's comes to mind; I read it years ago, when, as a pastor needing resources for ministry far above and beyond my own, I first became truly interested in prayer. I have written it out, preached it, quoted it in books. It seems so simple, what he said, but so precisely what I need right now: "It is faith that gives a [person] courage to pray.

It is this faith that gives him [or her] power to prevail with God. One great reason for lack of prayer is the [lack] of the living, joyous assurance: my God will hear me."[60]

And now something inside me rises up in joy. I pray again. And what a delight my intercessory prayers become. Instead of a duty, they are transformed into a fruitful encounter with the God who hears me. The assurance underneath and behind and supporting what I am doing fills me with a glow of eagerness. Not that I expect God to be subject to me, working only at my bidding call. But I know now, with renewed conviction, that he listens. God is actually glad to hear me talk!

∽

My insight does not exhaust the meaning of prayer, but it shoots me to the center of it: "We do not pray for the sake of praying," wrote Thomas Merton, "but for the sake of being heard. We do not pray in order to listen to ourselves praying but in order that God may hear us and answer us."[61] God does not invite us to pray, either, as an exercise in merely "unloading." He actually, eagerly wants us to come—to ask, seek, knock on his door.

A writer for a Bible project I recently supervised found a quote from the German spiritual writer Friedrich von Hügel: "If you but gently persevere through [the stress of dryness and darkness], you will come out at the other end of the gloom, sooner or later, into even deeper, tenderer day."[62]

And this has been happening for me. *So I will continue laying my requests before you, O God. So I will continue to wait—to wait for you in expectation.*

A Consuming Desire

Lord, let me seek you by wanting you,
  And let me want you by seeking you.
Let me find you by loving you,
  And by loving you, find you.
With thanks I acknowledge that you have made me in your image
  that I may remember you, think of you, and love you.
But that image has been so worn and eroded by faults,
  and shrouded by the smoke of sin,
  that it cannot do that for which it was made,
  unless you renew it and recreate it.

—ANSELM, *PROSLOGION*
(AUTHOR'S RENDERING)

HOW WELL DO I REMEMBER WHEN GOD first became real to me. It was not a trick of philosophy or a turn of argument that did it, that won me over. It was a sense, after a childhood of mostly routine church attendance, that Someone was there. That Christ was not distant, but near. I was not argued into love for God, but met, beckoned. I found my heart, as Methodism's founder John Wesley put it, "strangely warmed."

I was fourteen or so, and a mixture of longing and love and joy stirred in me when I began reading the Gospels and meeting Jesus heart-to-heart. What had previously been form and more or less religious routine became immediacy and intimacy. I still remember awaking in the sunshine of my house in a southern California suburb, aware that I could converse with a God no longer vague or distant or uncaring. How vivid did those weeks of first encounter seem!

Now, many years later, I find some of that same desire and discovery articulated in Anselm's prayer in his *Proslogion*.

> *Lord, let me seek you by wanting you,*
> *And let me want you by seeking you.*

So often we think of our devotion and prayer in terms of performance. But usually desire counts most. Our seeking is fueled by our wanting. And so I ask God this morning for help even in the desiring.

୧୨

> *Let me find you by loving you,*
> *And by loving you, find you.*

"We approach God through love," Augustine is purported to have said, "not navigation." Not through charts and day-planners and to-do lists, but by hearts that reach out in love and desire.

My mind keeps coming back to a retreat I led yesterday, to an insight one of the participants shared. At one point I had dismissed the retreatants from our meeting room. "Take time for some personal quiet and reflection," I said. "Walk the grounds or find a quiet corner in which to sit. Do what you like; just don't talk. Then we'll reconvene."

And I gave the same assignment I suggested to the campus ministers I spent a weekend with earlier this year: Reflect on Psalm 63, which articulates a keen desire for God. The first part of verse 1 reads:

O God, you are my God,
earnestly I seek you.

When we came back, I asked the group about their time with
the psalm. One woman reflected with a touch of wonder, "This
psalm was autobiographical for me." And I know enough of her
life—her deep alienation from her father, a bout with depression,
times when God seemed distant—to know why she might feel far
away, and yet long to return. Something in the psalm's poignant
cry moved her.

Another participant grew philosophical. "In my experience,"
he said, "we get a swallow or a taste, but that little bit only
increases our thirst. So we keep wanting more of God, and that
keeps us going."

I nodded. That sounds, I said, like the saying, "Don't pray for
water; pray for thirst." I think the saying is *half* right: We can and
should, after all, also pray for water. Living Water. Still, thirst—
spiritual desire—can be a great asset in the spiritual life. It can
keep us resolutely walking forward during the arid times, searching for the divine moisture our souls cannot do without. Not if
they are to thrive.

Anselm, I realize now as I pray, had a similar take on what we
want in prayer but do not possess. One of the Middle Ages' keen-
est minds, he devoted himself to the pursuit of truth. Many scholars put his contribution as a theologian/philosopher between
Augustine and Thomas Aquinas in the row of the world's great
thinkers. He loved rational arguments and immersion in the questions of Aristotle and other ancient philosophers. He seemed consumed with desire to understand God. He spent his powers of
reasoning trying to prove irrefutably that God existed.

But he also faced a profound realization of the limits of his thought, his will, his love. In his prayer I see a person who knows he cannot himself, for all his love of intellectual categories, figure out God. To experience God he knew he must not only think, but also desire. He would strive not only to understand, but also to open to One above all thought.

While we usually remember Anselm as a philosopher or theologian, he derived his primary identity from his vocation as a monk. The monastery made Anselm. Worship formed the rhythm of his days. Prayer was the daily air he breathed, loving devotion the spirit that infused his pursuit.

It is said of Anselm, I learn later, that one night a fellow monk was walking through the monastery, about to wake the others for prayer. He happened to pass the door of one of the meeting rooms and, Anselm's chronicler notes, "he looked in and saw Anselm standing in prayer in the midst of a great ball of blazing fire." Thinking he was having only a vision, the monk rushed over to Anselm's bed in the dormitory. Anselm was not there. The wide-eyed monk returned and found Anselm in the meeting room, "but without the ball of fire."[63]

Did Anselm's followers inflate a story here, laying over his life the medieval fascination with the miraculous (which our time shares)? Perhaps. But perhaps not. After all, here was a man whose longing would not stop at form or liturgy or classroom. Perhaps he literally *burned* with loving desire for God. God himself.

⚭

And so here I am, without such dramatic manifestations. At least today. But I can pray. I can seek God with my mind and my will and my heart and my soul. I can begin, when the wanting lacks the warmth of love, by asking for assistance. I can turn to God, ready for him to help me to want him more. To turn to One, the only one, who can slake my driving thirst.

I have to confess, like Anselm, that I, made in God's image, still witness the corrosive effects of my sin and my self-obsession and my forgetfulness. They obscure the clarity of that holy image. They daily, constantly, threaten my freedom in Christ and my passion for God. But again, I can pray. And again. I can come to God recognizing my need. God's image formed in me, I admit in prayer, *cannot do that for which it was made, unless you renew it and recreate it.* I cannot even think straight, unless God comes. I cannot put my affections in order without divine guidance. I will not love right, unless God helps. But the God I want to love loves me even more profoundly. He will hear, and understand, and move to help when I ask:

> *Let me find you by loving you,*
> *And by loving you, find you.*

Taking Prayer Seriously

O, my God, if one knew the value of prayer, the great advantage that comes to the soul from talking with you, and what consequence it is of to salvation, everyone would be diligent in it. Prayer is a fortification into which the enemy may never enter. The enemy may attack it, besiege it, create a commotion around its walls; but while we are faithful and stay at our battle station, the Devil cannot hurt us.

—MADAME GUYON
(AUTHOR'S RENDERING)

LAST NIGHT MY FRIEND KEVIN CALLED TO tell me about a book he was reading—the autobiography of the seventeenth century French mystic Jeanne-Marie Bouvier de la Motte-Guyon (better known as Madame Guyon). He told me about an experience Madame Guyon had had as a young adult, something that struck him as he read. She had decided, Kevin recounted, not to spend time in spontaneous prayer (also known as "mental" prayer). Instead, she would use a prescribed "office," that is, pattern, of prayer. She did not have time for both kinds of prayer, she reasoned, and a suitor was also going to be saying the prayer office. She wanted to join him to try it.

The results were disastrous, Kevin told me. Guyon soon realized how vital it was to converse freely with God, not to stint when it came to time in his presence. "The devil," she would later write, "is outrageous only against prayer, and those that exercise it; because he knows it is the true means of taking his prey from him."[64]

My friend's admiration for the writings of this French woman, imprisoned for her willingness to stand against the religious authorities of her day, stirred me, too. But I think Kevin also had in mind suggesting a correction to my tendency to highlight the rewards of praying. I prefer to reassure and invite rather than warn when speaking of prayer, but Madame Guyon not only extolled prayer, but also got honest about the cost it may exact. She knew taking prayer seriously could mean difficulties, ridicule, even persecution. Give yourself to a life of prayer, she wrote, and prepare for hardship. I think my friend Kevin, cultivating a deeper interest in prayer, was sobered by that. As was I.

"The road to hell," someone once said, shortening the familiar saying, "is paved." That is, it is a road made smooth and deceptively inviting. Whereas that other way, of which Jesus said, "Narrow [is] the road that leads to life, and only a few find it" (Matthew 7:14), is fraught with rocky spots and hazards and detours. And I think that is something of what Madame Guyon meant. Beware, she seems to say, if prayer looms only as light and consolation and warmth. The real thing hurts sometimes. Prayer is a battle. Get ready for "strange crosses." She wrote, "All manner of persecutions and contempts in this world are reserved for that life."[65]

I had to find out more about her.

∾

For all her discussion of the costs of a prayerful life, I found, Madame Guyon also inspired readers with the promise of its joys. And not just superficial satisfactions. Not given the life she lived, with more than a dozen years of captivity, with constant suspicion about her beliefs from her church superiors. While thoroughly Catholic, she would soon become beloved by Protestants who admired her bucking of some of the excesses of Catholic piety. But she did so at extreme personal cost. And also with great personal stamina, even rapturous delight.

O, my God, if the value of prayer were truly known, the great advantage that comes to the soul from talking with you, and what consequence it is of to salvation, everyone would be diligent in it. I wonder, *Why do I so easily forget what strength is to be found here?* "Prayer," someone once said, "is not preparation for the important work. It *is* the important work." Prayer is not something that I turn to when I think I "need" emotional bolstering. It takes me to the source of any and everything I enjoy or know or experience. Even I—the writer on prayer, the one who talks about the importance of prayer, who thinks about a ministry devoted to prayer and nurturing prayer in others—how prayerless some of my days seem! How little, sometimes, do I act on my belief that the day is won not by ingenuity or street savvy or dogged persistence, but through radically constant, simple, yielding prayer.

I think of something I read some years ago, an image that comes back to mind every now and then. Haddon Robinson, then homiletics professor at Gordon-Conwell Seminary, once talked of how, for Jesus, prayer formed the center of the battle. It was where all ground was truly gained. "Where was it that Jesus sweat great drops of blood?" asks Robinson. "Not in Pilate's Hall, nor on his way to Golgotha. It was in the Garden of Gethsemene [where he prayed and awaited his death]. . . . Had I been there and witnessed that struggle, I would have worried about the future. 'If he is so broken up when all he is doing is praying,' I might have said, 'what will he do when he faces a real crisis? Why can't he approach this ordeal with the calm confidence of his three sleeping friends?' Yet, when the test came, Jesus walked to the cross with courage, and his three friends fell away."[66] It was not easy, but prayer made all the difference.

~

I could stand to believe this more. So I take the words of Madame Guyon and turn them back to God: *Prayer is a fortification into which the enemy cannot enter, Lord. The enemy may attack it, besiege it, create a commotion around its walls; but while we are faithful and stay at our battle station, the Devil cannot hurt us.* The Devil cannot hurt *me*.

Lord make it so. Or rather, let me see that it is so, already, so that I will not take prayer lightly—when I teach about it, when I write about it, and especially when I actually manage to pray.

I have a long way to go in this life of prayer. But at least I see the promises, luring me on. At least I see some of prayer's possibilities, keeping me going, keeping me at it, even when it costs me.

Drenched in Mercy

O great Father,
Great is our need,
And so we beseech you now
Bring your Word
Through which you filled us
With what we lacked;
Let it please you now, Father—
For it is fitting—
To look upon us
In case we fail
And your name is darkened within us,
Which is our help in need.[67]

—HILDEGARD OF BINGEN

I BEGAN TO BE AWARE OF HILDEGARD OF Bingen in more than a cursory way Wednesday night. At my church, at our weekly informal prayer and praise service, our interim pastor, Paul Nancarrow, told us much about Hildegard.

She was born in 1098, he said, meaning this year of my apprenticeship to the great spiritual mentors marks the nine hundredth anniversary of her birth. And in Germany, where she was born, great celebrations unfold. People turn with fascination and eager curiosity to a woman who lived almost a millennia ago, leading an abbey on the banks of the Rhine River.

Paul spoke about how amazing her varied accomplishments were—how popes consulted with her, all the more unusual because she was a woman. How she created music, still recorded to this day. ("Music wakes us from our sluggishness," she said to a sister in her abbey.) Most fascinating of all, perhaps, were her Illuminations— vivid paintings of the visions she believed came from God, of which Paul had made pale reproductions from an Internet site, projecting them on a screen for us to enjoy. These visions highlighted the grand themes of faith: Creation, the Fall, redemption. Hildegard claimed to be unlettered, but her writings spread far and wide. She was, one historian notes, "taken seriously as a prophet by everyone, from Bernard of Clairvaux and the pope down to the humblest laborers."[68]

ꙮ

Today I say Hildegard's prayer, not singing antiphonally, as it was first intended (the title is "Antiphon for God the Father," suggesting it was composed for liturgical worship), but I try to enter its rhythms of worship and devotion nevertheless.

Right off I see how drenched with awareness of God's grace (and our need for it) these verses seem. From childhood, Hildegard was often sick, sometimes debilitatingly so. Migraines apparently left her unable even to walk at times. Perhaps there in the convent of nuns, under whose care she came at age seven or eight, and which she formally joined at age fourteen, perhaps in that austere, self-denying atmosphere common to medieval religious communities, Hildegard learned firsthand how to turn to God in extremity and need:

> *And so we beseech you now*
> *Bring your Word*

Through which you filled us
With what we lacked. . . .

She, who loved to write and compose and create, knew that ultimately God alone fills us with his Word and life. *And so I beseech you now, myself, O Lord. Please, come and fill me in what I lack.*

Hildegard, for all her notoriety and esteemed influence, knew what it meant to fail. Seen by some as domineering, even manipulative, she knew well her inescapable need for mercy.

For it is fitting—
To look upon us
In case we fail
And your name is darkened within us,
Which is our help in need.

༖

As happens so often with a prayer, I find myself not simply appreciating its insight, but needing its articulation of my true condition. *In case we fail!* I know well that I do. *And your name is darkened within us.*

This morning I sat in darkness, felt it vividly. I had lit a candle during my early morning prayer time, hoping it would remind me, when my mind wanted to wander, what I was about. When I blew it out, darkness fell indeed. Just as my life grows sometimes dim and dark in forgetfulness of God.

But what mercy is here, too! As the modern poet Jane Kenyon writes while facing her fatal cancer, "God, as promised, proves to be mercy clothed in light."[69] Hildegard knew this. And she reminds me of it this morning. As the darkness turns to light and the day begins.

Astonished by Glory

No one is like you, O Lord;
you are great,
and your name is mighty in power.
Who should not revere you,
O King of the nations?
This is your due.
Among all the wise men of the nations
and in all their kingdoms,
there is none like you.

—JEREMIAH, THE PROPHET

SOMETIMES, LIKE TODAY, I NEED HELP SEEING reality for what it is. I perceive my life only for what it seems at the hurried moment. I get caught up in my tasks, sometimes caught up in myself. I become oblivious to the backdrop of God's subtle markers of presence and glory.

Rolling out of bed, packing Bekah's lunch, sitting down to write, paying the bills, running to the store, watching my cholesterol, hoping my work is successful, pulling out a novel at bedtime—such are the involvements that largely define today. These are the responsibilities I shoulder, the promises I have to keep. These are the little joys and everyday matters. And they *do* matter.

But I don't want them to squeeze out my view of a holy realm of light and illumination and beauty. I don't want concrete and backed-up cars and a carpet crying out to be vacuumed to obscure a larger dimension. I want all this to point me to a glory hidden in a universe made and sustained by an infinite God.

In the book I wrote just before beginning this year of prayer, I described my efforts to watch for "traces of God in the corners and crevices of an ordinary nine-to-five."[70] I still work at it. "How many common things," wrote Augustine, "are trodden underfoot which, when examined carefully, awaken our astonishment."[71] I began the book with that quote; I am still learning to put it into practice.

The prayer that shapes this week helps me show up for it all not with dulled eyes and blurry vision, but with a determination to ponder—even notice in the first place—what lies beyond and above my little world and infiltrates all of life. In church every Sunday, one of the ancient prayers of Christian worship we sing is "Sanctus":

> *Holy, holy, holy, Lord, God of Power and Might*
> *Heaven and earth are full of your glory!*

And when I slow down enough to really look, I see a towering maple, leaves an autumn lemon-yellow fire, that in itself is a wonder of complexity and chemical process and exorbitant beauty. I see a God-saturated world!

Heaven and earth are full! God did not have to make it so glorious. But he did. And while earth itself is a wonder, a constant advertisement to a glory that would beggar my wildest imaginings, there is yet another realm. The prophet Isaiah described it in his vision:

> *In the year that King Uzziah died, I saw the Lord seated on a throne, high and exalted, and the train of his robe filled the temple.*

Above him were seraphs, each with six wings: With two wings they
covered their faces, with two they covered their feet, and with two
they were flying. And they were calling to one another:
  *"Holy, holy, holy is the L*ORD *Almighty;*
  the whole earth is full of his glory." (Isaiah 6:1–3)

When I read these words, my internal eyes snap to attention at a realm just beyond physical sight but full of reality for
my every moment. The seraphs, strange heavenly, angelic
beings who, filled with a sense of overpowering wonder, are
reduced to simple speech and awe-struck worship in the presence of God.

And Jeremiah's prayer tells me where to stop looking in vain
and where, for the good of my soul, to fix the eyes of my heart.
Who else is like you, O God?

Who else, indeed?

∽

Part of it, I see right off, has to do with my picture of God. *Holy,*
holy, holy. A God who is radically, unfathomably *Other.* So
immeasurably holy, permeated with a kind of goodness
untouched by anything base, that the heavenly beings in Isaiah's
vision repeat the word again and again. *Holy, holy, holy.* A God so
powerfully glorious that the heavenly beings in the vision had to
cover their faces. A Presence so astonishingly clean of any defile-
ment that they had to cover their feet for fear that they would
tread into the realm of unfathomable purity. *No one is like you, O*
Lord. You are great.

Such is the drama of heaven. Such is the world that carries on
unseen, just barely hidden from view. We get glimpses from the

Bible, perhaps even from a rare personal experience. But I need to be coaxed to open my eyes.

C. S. Lewis tells of how he struggled, when he first became a believer, with the idea of God's "deserving" praise, of God's "right" to be praised. It seemed odd for God to expect from us a "perpetual eulogy," Lewis said.

He found help in an analogy.

> What do we mean when we say that a picture is "admirable"? We certainly don't mean that it is admired . . . for bad work is admired by thousands and good work may be ignored. Nor that it "deserves" admiration in the sense in which a candidate "deserves" a high mark from the examiners. . . . The sense in which the picture "deserves" or "demands" admiration is rather this; that admiration is the correct, adequate or appropriate response to it, that, if paid, admiration will not be "thrown away," and that if we do not admire we shall be stupid, insensible, and great losers, we shall have missed something. . . . [God] is that Object to admire which (or, if you like, to appreciate which) is simply to be awake, to have entered the real world."[72]

So I will keep coming to God, as I can, with praise. For in fleeting moments—out running, singing in church, sitting quietly in prayer—I get flashes of awareness of a Glory so compelling that I know were I to look on it with my physical eyes I would have to turn my face away. Out of the corner of my soul's eye is about all I can handle. Perhaps it is God's grace indeed that I do not see more of his incomparable splendor. Could I see God and live?

But with what I do see and know, what response can be appropriate except to honor and bless and praise? The words are pale next to the reality, but still they arise from within. Still they are called for even when the feelings do not gush out. Still they are Another's due in a universe of wonders.

Though my culture would tell me that God is ethereal and that physical things are what truly matter, it is when I see and sense God that I connect with the "real world." Though the world would tell me that my own wants and impatient needs can fill my life, my prophet pray-ers remind me otherwise.

This week, underneath my repeating of these great prayers of earlier centuries, runs a longing for a heart that lives and sings in the unseen realm of the real. For eyes to recognize at least glimpses of a God who blazes in a heavenly light I can see only dimly. For words that begin to honor God with the praise of which he is worthy.

Dry Soul, Dark Night

My soul grows dry because it forgets to feed on you.
—JOHN OF THE CROSS

LAST NIGHT I JOINED A COUPLE OF DOZEN people for a house-warming party and home dedication. I could not have predicted the kind of conversation I would soon find myself immersed in.

Cynthia, the youth minister at my church, hosted the gathering in her tiny house in a more-or-less new neighborhood of Nashville, and the place felt crowded and festive. The service of blessing led by our pastor reminded us all—youth, parents, neighbors—of how God plants his presence in our lives wall-to-wall, room-by-room. Then the party began.

As did my conversation with Rob (not his real name), a volunteer with the youth group. Despite the milling, exuberant guests, and even though Rob and I sat cross-legged on the living room floor near heavy refreshment traffic, the conversation moved into deep waters. Rob told me with little preamble that he had been struggling emotionally and spiritually—a romantic relationship had just ended, the third to end within two years with the woman wanting out. Rob was well into his thirties, and marriage seemed more elusive than ever, his emotions that much more bruised. Just as bad, God seemed far away.

"I've gotten really mad at God," he told me. "Part of me has felt at times that God has not kept his end of the 'bargain.' It's been rough."

I did a great deal of listening, of course. And empathizing. But the conversation soon shifted in tone. Rob told me of some drastic growth the pain had begun to exact. "I recently read in the book of Hosea," he said, "of how God tore the people to pieces in order that he might heal." This is not how I am used to picturing God. Nor was Rob. "But," he said, "I realize that *God* is working in my life through all that's happening, and while it's painful, while I have to wrestle, I'm going deeper with God through all of this."

I mentioned to Rob how I had been reading of the sixteenth-century Spanish writer, John of the Cross. He is perhaps best known for his phrase, also the title of one of his books, "the dark night of the soul." I told Rob that John spoke of such a time as one in which the normal comforts and even spiritual warmth vanish. The world seems dark, the soul dry. Rob nodded. I could tell that the metaphor of a dark night and dry soul resonated deeply.

At home I looked up the passage in Hosea he had mentioned, this stark passage about a prophet who invites, "Come, let us return to the LORD; for it is he who has torn, and he will heal us; he has struck down, and he will bind us up, that we might live before him" (Hosea 6:1).

And I thought, *Rob is going to be okay.*

I also made a mental note to turn again to the writings of John of the Cross—for myself. For I know that too often I am dry. Part of that may, of course, never change. The life I lead, even with God in it, is not all moist warmth and luxuriant light. Sometimes faith requires sheer determination. There are dark nights in the desert. So if I am to learn to know and love God alone, John would tell me, and Rob, we must learn to let go of our earthly loves and luxuries. We must hold lightly the niceties, forgo the expectation that even prayer will always seem wonderfully, wildly fulfilling. We grow up in our relationship with God. And we come to a mid-life of the soul. Only then, John said, can we grow more deeply, profoundly in love with God.

∽

This morning I awoke feeling anxious for Bekah, who is having trouble letting go of us some mornings when we drop her off at school. I am troubled over my wife's struggles in her job, situated as she is on a staff of a church embroiled in heated, painful combat. Whole families are leaving the church. Hard, harsh words are being said. These things are hard to witness. And yesterday brought disappointing news for me from two people I hoped would write endorsements for my newest book; they sent regrets instead, citing their already too-full schedules. I understood, but still found it hard not to see the responses as rejections. I found myself riding down a spiral of self-doubt, even questioning my calling.

There were other moments yesterday, though. Moments I could see my work and my routine, my making phone calls and planning supper, as *enough,* because I could see in them as more than tasks to accomplish, as occasions for communion with God as well. I didn't need fame or fortune during those truer moments. I was able to say to God, "Overseeing my career is your job; even as I do my best, it's ultimately in your hands, not mine."

I did not expect ecstasies, only quiet peace. I could just be me, just be *God's.* And while waiting in the car to bring Bekah home from school, I came across this prayer of John of the Cross's, in a book of prayers I grabbed just before leaving the house.

My soul grows dry because it forgets to feed on you.[73]

I began praying John's words immediately. They remind me that I need God more than I need a predictable or cozy life. I need Presence more than pleasure. I need not to be acclaimed, but held by an embrace that outlasts any accolades. I will not be content until I make that, and continue to make that, my focus.

And even during the times I seem not so aware of God, I find they too have their consolations. Psychologist James Hillman suggests that "absence is the first form of knowing." I'm not sure it is the *first* form, but it is our lack of a sense of presence that, paradoxically, confirms that the presence exists. God comes close, I realize, not just when I sense him vividly, but even in those times he may seem far away, times my soul in its dryness has to utter praise and petitions with a cotton-mouth tongue and a fatigued heart. Even the sense of his absence points to what was once vivid Presence; what will, I trust, once again be sweet communion.

∾

The struggle continues another day. This morning I had trouble again dropping off Bekah at second grade. She fought me loudly about going to school—even at the curbside when it was time for her to go in. I felt embarrassed. I came back demolished emotionally. Jill said something about our needing to put the situation in God's hands, and I cut her off. "You make it sound so easy!" I snapped. And then I poured out all my other frustrations as well.

Jill lovingly encouraged me to try something she was trying: to spend time meditating on John 10:10, where Jesus says: "I came that they may have life, and have it abundantly" (NRSV). Why not, she suggested, use it as part of my prayer time? So I took the dog for a walk, praying as I rounded our block, the October morning air already cooling, the trees glinting red tints and orange fire. And as I sat at my desk later, I prayed through the morning for guidance. For the abundance God wants to bring. I tried to let go of my own clenched convictions of the way things should turn out. Why not let God surround me with the peace of himself—so much better than the superficial satisfaction of "happy" circumstances? I reminded myself of what Jesus promised life could be.

And as the day went on, things seemed more in place. I wasn't as discouraged.

෮

Yet another morning. I think about John of the Cross—a gifted poet, writer, spiritual director. He knew the reality of a dark night of the soul; his books *The Dark Night of the Soul* and *The Ascent of Mount Carmel* reveal an intimate familiarity with the struggles of prayerfulness. He offered no glib assumption along the lines of the bumper sticker, "Don't feel close to God? Guess who moved?" No, he knew that faithfulness inevitably included times when an unstintingly sunshiny smile would not hold. More was needed during the harrowing times when plans fall apart, when God seems not to care like we first thought. What is needed is the conviction that God is not fickle; he promises to never leave or forsake us. But neither does God want us addicted to spiritual "warm fuzzies." God may withdraw his consolations, as the old spiritual writers call the tangible interior benefits we sometimes gain in prayer.

John also knew that dryness sometimes results from our own inattention to God, our forgetfulness of the Lord and his many benefits. I don't know how much my desolation this week comes from God's weaning me from superficial affections. Surely some of it comes from my own sloppy habits. But I know that the problem is not that God is gone. And so that is what I will try to pray my way out of today.

Whatever happens this week, wherever I go, whether I see a glorious sunrise or a storm on the horizon, my soul will not go bereft. My dry spirit will find sustenance. God will lead my dry soul to still waters, day or night.

Staying Power

I need thee ev'ry hour, most gracious Lord;
No tender voice like thine can peace afford.
I need thee, Oh I need thee, ev'ry hour I need thee!
Oh bless me now, my Savior, I come to thee.

I need thee ev'ry hour, in joy or pain;
Come quickly, and abide, or life is vain.
I need thee, Oh I need thee; ev'ry hour I need thee!
Oh bless me now my Savior, I come to thee.

I need thee ev'ry hour, teach me thy will,
And thy rich promises in me fulfill.
I need thee, Oh I need thee; ev'ry hour I need thee!
Oh bless me now, my Savior, I come to thee.

—Annie Hawks

I HAVE A LITTLE PAPERBACK THAT COLLECTS hymn texts for people to use in devotional times. This prayer hymn, filled with evangelical fervor and piety, caught my eye as I looked through the book. How many times have I sung it in church over the years! The hymn has spread far beyond its nineteenth-century Baptist American origins. And now, a century and a quarter after the lyrics seemed simply to present themselves to a young Brooklyn woman, it speaks to me. It reminds me of the source of anything that really matters. It helps me pray.

In 1873, Annie Hawks, at the age of thirty-seven, tended the needs of her family and stayed active at Hanson Place Baptist Church. Nothing much remarkable about her life, you could say. But then, as she described it:

> One day as a young wife and mother, I was busy with my regular household tasks during a bright June morning, in 1872. Suddenly, I became filled with the awareness of the nearness of the Master, and I began to wonder how anyone could live without Him, either in joy or in pain. Then some words were ushered into my mind and these thoughts took full possession of me.

So came the words to this now-famous hymn. She took them to the pastor of her church, an accomplished composer. He put music with the words and added a refrain. The hymn quickly became popular. But Annie would find the message of the hymn she wrote coming back to her in an unexpected way.

Sixteen years later, Annie's husband died, an event that left her heartbroken and that led her to a new insight:

> I did not understand at first why [my] hymn had touched the great heart of humanity. It was not until . . . the shadow fell over my way, the shadow of great loss, that I understood something of the comforting power in the words, which I had been permitted to give out to others in my hour of sweet serenity and peace.

And so, this prayer reminds me, in my high moments of joy this week, my low junctures of disappointment, and, most commonly, the middle stretch that much of life becomes day after day, I *need* God. "We see," says an art commentator, "only what we look for in need." While he was commenting on the human experience of appreciating a painting or sculpture, much the same truth, I find, can apply to faith.

Perhaps it should not be this way, but my lacks often send me in search of what God can give. This week's uncertainties make me prone to turn to what God can make of them. They help me remember that God is not some hobby or occasional indulgence, like a cup of gourmet coffee or favorite movie I might put in the VCR at the end of a day. No, prayer is an hourly proposition if for no other reason than that our need, our joy, our hope is an hourly proposition. And only in God can I muster anything resembling staying power.

So I pray,

> *I need thee ev'ry hour, most gracious Lord;*
> *No tender voice like thine can peace afford.*
> *I need thee, Oh I need thee, ev'ry hour I need thee!*
> *Oh bless me now, my Savior, I come to thee.*

And here, I find, the substance of hope. *I need thee, Oh I need thee, ev'ry hour I need thee!*

∾

And here I also find the antidote to despair. Thomas Merton helps me in this regard also. Because our own human resources inevitably fail us, he wrote, "We are all more or less subject to discouragement and to despair" unless we let our limitations drive us to God. When we do, however, we "thereby acknowledge that He is above us and that we are not capable of fulfilling our destiny by ourselves."[74] And there we learn again that he is sovereign. That nothing lies outside his sight. Nothing is ultimately futile. Not when it leads us back to him.

Come quickly, and abide, or life is vain, I pray. And then grace can come flooding in.

Grace *is* flooding in. Thanks be to God.

Childlike Faith

Father we thank you for the night
And for the pleasant morning light,
For rest and food and loving care,
And all that makes the day so fair.

Help us to do the things we should
To be to others kind and good
In all we do, and all we say,
And to grow more loving every day.[75]

—REBECCA J. WESTON

BEKAH READ THIS AT THE TABLE LAST NIGHT for our prayer before supper. I've been collecting table graces to use at family meal times, typing and cutting them into small cards that rest in a brass box that sits no more than three inches tall, easily kept on the kitchen counter or dining-room table.

Meal-time prayer is a simple discipline. We don't always pull out a printed prayer. Often one of us will simply say a quick word of thanks for the food and one another. But every now and then we draw out a card with a prayer that stretches our customary words. Usually Bekah, as the youngest, is the one to read it. She takes pride in doing so, just as she enjoyed helping me record them by reading them aloud as I sat at the computer and typed them up. And, I think, these words that she may not always jump at reading, may sometimes even stumble over, will train her mind and teach her the rhythms of devotion.

∽

So this week it is a prayer for a child, even said out loud *by* a child, that guides me.

After the high-flying spiritual theology of John of the Cross or the severity of Thomas à Kempis, I like the freshness of the prayer's childlike delight, its reveling in simple blessings. It reminds me of the goodness of creation. It reminds me that caring for others matters more than the anxieties that shadow my everyday occupations.

And today a little girl leads me. I gain help in my efforts to be faithful by recognizing goodness through the eyes (and voice) of a child. A childlike prayer reminds me how grounded even lofty matters are in simple blessings. A universe of great extravagance and unimaginably far reaches and untold wonders, paradoxically, often elicits more awe in a small child than it does in a sophisticated adult. And so I learn childlike ways.

∽

Yesterday at church I taught a class on nurturing faith in children. Even a small child, I reminded the class of parents, possesses an inborn spiritual sensitivity, or at least the potential for it. Much of children's spiritual awareness seems to be something simply *there,* an impulse to worship and thank God planted in them by the One whose creative hand brought them into the world. Some of it has to do with the newness with which they experience everything. They feel the world up close, taste its sensations with unbridled abandon. But part of it simply seems to be that the building blocks for astonishment and compassion grow in little souls. Often we learn from *them*. Jesus, I reminded them, said, "I praise you, Father, Lord of heaven and earth, because you have hidden these [insights] from the wise and learned, and revealed them to little children" (Matthew 11:25).

∾

One man who attended the class told me of taking a walk with his son Aidan. Suddenly Paul noticed his son's absence. He looked around, finally looked *behind,* and there was Aidan, resolutely uninterested in hurrying along. The boy crouched on someone's lawn, oblivious to his dad's urgent pace. And when Paul asked with exasperation what he was doing, Aidan said simply, "I'm praying with the clover."

So I will pray thanks over the lasagna tonight. I will try, when walking to the end of the driveway to get the paper tomorrow morning, to notice the flash of a red cardinal in the morning sunshine. I will let the silhouetted trees on the hill across the valley and the smile of my wife and even the list of calls I face become an occasion to remember God. With gratitude.

Waiting on God

Out of the depths I cry to you, O Lord;
O Lord, hear my voice.
Let your ears be attentive
  to my cry for mercy.
If you, O Lord, kept a record of sins,
  O Lord, who could stand?
But with you there is forgiveness;
  therefore you are feared.
I wait for the Lord, my soul waits,
  and in his word I put my hope.
My soul waits for the Lord
  more than watchmen wait for the morning,
  more than watchmen wait for the morning.
                    —DAVID, THE PSALMIST

DURING THIS TIME OF INTENSE PRAYER
about my vocation, I turn to a "Song of Ascents," one of
the "Pilgrim Psalms" that were sung by those who traveled (and
thus "ascended") to the temple for the annual feasts. Each of these
songs is a "step" along the journey. And I am definitely on a journey, trying to find my way "up" into clarity of God's calling on my
life. The word *vocation*, I remember reading once, comes from a
Latin word that means to give a bidding or invitation. A vocation

is doing what we are invited to do, what is ours to do. And I am smack in the middle of a time of discerning what that is.

Monday night I met with the group charged by my denomination with helping to test and sort through my call to ministry. In my answers to the questions asked of all candidates, I told the group something of my own sense of re-emerging call. In recent years, I wrote in my introductory material,

> and particularly in recent months, I have sensed a profound and persistent stirring to return to pastoral ministry. In a way this new sense of calling has been percolating for a long time. In another way it crystallized for me just a few months ago as I heard my pastor teach an adult Sunday school class on worship. As I watched him in action, I felt a sudden clarity that I should pursue ordination, this time in my "new" denomination.

Of course, I said, I know that God's call can take many forms. Ordained ministry is certainly not the only one. I told them some of my story, too, from my sense of calling to ministry as a high schooler, to a sense of calling to editing and writing as a young adult, and now, in my early forties, a sense that it was time to bring both aspects of those aptitudes and interests together.

The seven of us shared our spiritual autobiographies. Each member of the group, only one a member of the clergy, told of his own tracing of God's hand in his life. Several also asked questions about how their work lives relate to their faith walk.

And the focus shifted once again to me. I knew going in that most of the people in the group were warmly supportive of my ministry. But to my surprise, the tone of the meeting pushed me a bit. One questioned why, if I was already engaged in a fruitful ministry of writing and retreat leading, I would *need* ordination.

Suddenly I felt a greater burden to prove the force of my call. I felt caught off guard. I realized this group is going to push me to do more than rely on vague impressions or perhaps-imagined nudges. The challenges over these next few months of the discernment process may ask more from me than I expected. I realize how living my vocation sometimes means taking the harder path. It may mean doing what people question, sometimes even criticize. How I identify with anyone taking a risk when it comes to his or her job or career or place in life!

෨෨

This morning, as the tasks of my current calling make their urgencies felt, I find myself having trouble letting go of the meeting last night and the prospect of months of further meetings with the committee. Anxiety is creeping in. Perhaps also a bit of hurt. Why can't this process shower me with unbridled praise, as though I am God's favored gift to the church?

I don't know that I can claim to have to pray out of the "depths," as this week's psalm has it. I am not facing a tragic loss or catastrophic medical diagnosis or rupture of faith. But this morning's prayer time has put me in touch with vague restlessness. And it has brought me back, so to speak, into a sense of the rightness of things and the goodness of God.

And a book I am reading about the insights of Julian of Norwich has helped as well. The fourteenth-century spiritual writer, as the author put it, "recognized our propensity to be disorientated from God, and therefore saw the need to take whatever measures necessary to heal the fracture within us, bringing our external self . . . into line with our true self or substance in union with God."[76]

For Julian, of course, that meant immersion in the life of a solitary nun. She had chosen solitude and silence and likely the typical monastic vows of poverty, chastity, and obedience. She was willing to go to great lengths in order for God to have a larger, healing role in her life and through her life. "But," the historian notes, "the whole emphasis is on developing calmly and joyfully, finding the inner liberty that allows one to be wholly attentive to God and to others, rather than on a cramping of talent or happiness. . . . Because she had given herself wholly to God, she was able to take wholesome delight in the works of God and give whole-hearted attention to those who came to her."[77]

But what of our negative feelings? What of my tendency to dislike myself or grow irritated with my failings? What of my anxieties and moments of unsettleness, like today? What of those times I feel "in the depths"? Julian would say, "We are to acknowledge our negative feelings, own up to them and to the behavior which has caused them and expressed them unwisely or hurtfully to ourselves and others. Having owned up to them, however, we are to 'quickly pass over,' turning from mulling over our feelings to the steadiness of [God's] love and longing for us."[78]

❦

And so I find myself this morning turning to God and willing to wait for his goodness to be manifest in my questions and concerns for the future and the nagging sense of God's calling me again into ministry. Why should I worry?

> But with you there is forgiveness;
> therefore you are feared.

"There is that near you," wrote an old Quaker seeker, "that will guide you. Wait for it, and be sure to keep to it." He might have better said, "There is *One* near you . . . a loving, guiding *God* near you." What more matters?

I tend to want things immediately. In our age of microwave instancy, I don't necessarily think I should have to delay a deeper awareness of God or wait on a clear direction for my future work-day arena. But in some things, like growing my soul, a patient waiting is the most fruitful attitude. Opening to a God of love, confessing my faults, receiving his forgiveness—it cannot be otherwise. "We do not obtain the most precious gifts by going in search of them but by waiting for them," writes Simone Weil, a twentieth-century philosopher and spiritual life writer.[79]

By waiting for them. That is because we do not manufacture grace. We *receive* it. And so I will wait, today, and tomorrow, and the next day. I will resolve, whatever turns my discernment process for ministry takes, to say,

> *I wait for the Lord, my soul waits,*
> *and in his word I put my hope.*
> *My soul waits for the Lord*
> *more than watchmen wait for the morning,*
> *more than watchmen wait for the morning.*

The Source of Everlasting Blessing

> Blessing and Brightness
> Wisdom, thanksgiving,
> Great power and might
> To the King who rules over all.
> Glory and honor and goodwill,
> Praise and the sublime song of minstrels,
> Overflowing love from every heart
> To the King of Heaven and Earth.
> To the chosen Trinity has been joined
> Before all, after all, universal
> Blessing and everlasting blessing,
> Blessing everlasting and blessing.[80]
>
> —IRISH HYMN

THIS MORNING I HAVE FOUND THAT WORDS of glorious faith and spiritual declaration are not springing naturally to my lips. I have felt decidedly unlike praising God. In fact, I have not felt much of *anything*.

But I take comfort and direction from this prayer-hymn from the ninth century, realizing that I can pray it even with no great surge welling up. I need to get the words out and assume the feelings may follow, rather than the other way around. And even if great leaps of emotion do not come in the saying, this morning I will pray as this prayer reminds me I should. I will say the words by faith, not sentiment. I will align my thoughts with reality, not expect reality to conform to my feeling-flavor-of-the-hour.

"Feelings," Eugene Peterson wrote in a passage I have never forgotten, "are the scourge of prayer. To pray by feelings is to be at the mercy of glands and weather and indigestion. And there is no mercy in any of them."[81] This prayer of the Irish a millennium ago assures me that I will get out what needs to be gotten out, no matter my disposition on a rainy October morning.

As old as it is, this prayer-hymn has roots even more ancient. It picks up on the glorious scene of Revelation, given to John in a vision early in the church's life. He is given to see all the angels and living creatures and elders standing around the throne of God. This is no glib triumph; the scene follows visions in chapter six of death "by sword, famine and plague, and by the wild beasts of the earth." We gain glimpses of martyrdom, of stars falling from the heavens. And yet the angels and believers fall on their faces and worship God, saying:

> "Amen!
> Praise and glory
> and wisdom and thanks and honor
> and power and strength
> be to our God for ever and ever.
> Amen!" (Revelation 7:12)

John's visions fed the writer of this week's prayer, centuries ago. And now that prayer in turn feeds me. How small my frame of reference without such a bracing vision!

In the book where I have found this week's prayer, the author, Esther de Waal, comments on this and so many other prayers from the Celtic tradition—how, she says, they do not so much expect God to do something for us, as "They recognize what is already there, already given, waiting to be seen, to be taken up, enjoyed."[82] And certainly *worshiped.* Praise is prayer that does not demand but rather simply acknowledges what is good, and the Source of all that is good, the ultimate triumph of God. Says de Waal, "What a waste to go through life surrounded by all the good gifts that God showers on me, 'gently and generously' yet blind and deaf to his presence hidden in all things, human and nonhuman. . . . In the face of such amazing grace and generosity, the only possible response must become that of continuing and ever-deepening praise."[83]

I try to take the lesson to heart. Again.

ເ∾

Another day. I realize that praise of this sort is exactly what is called for as I walk through the hours ahead. I remember an article I read recently about how novelist Larry Woiwode would go walking as a twelve-year-old, often for miles at a time. He loved to walk the woods between his grandparents' house and a lake.

The latticework of shadow from the hedge-apple rows thickened to trunks and overarching shadows of trees—tall elms . . . maples, burr oaks all gnarled, horse chestnut, and a dozen other varieties our science teacher had pointed out on a field trip when I was so overwhelmed by the trees themselves I couldn't take in their names. . . .

I felt so much at home I sang as I sang nowhere else, sometimes mere notes that I felt began to reach the tones and patterns of plainsong. . . ."Oh, beautiful trees!" I sang. "Oh, sky above me! Oh, earth beneath my feet!" It was really a shout, blasts of assurance, the same song I sang each time I walked, as if to announce my presence to the elements I addressed— the sky and earth that had seemed to govern my life from its beginning. . . .

One presence was here, I saw, as I turned with my face raised, in the trees and sky and the earth that supported me as I turned. This presence had put all this in place to teach me about myself and its own qualities and makeup: *God.* I had been instructed to love Him, but the words of English I knew couldn't approach the language pouring from everything around with a familiarity that aroused in me a wordless love that for the life of me I couldn't define.[84]

Such stirrings awakened by the world around us point us to a world above us. To praise a *King who rules over all. . . . the King of Heaven and Earth.*

༄

And the Trinity! I can barely fathom the truth that God, one God and God alone, exists as a loving fellowship of three. Father, Son, and Holy Spirit all deserve my praise. In one sense the Trinity represents a theological truth, an articulation that helps us understand a complex reality. In another, profounder sense it is the language of reverence. It invites us to worship. In the presence of such brightness and blessing, indeed, even in glimpsing it faintly, what can I do but praise?

"If we have no real interest in praising [God]," I read in de Waal's book,

It shows that we have never realized who He is. For when one becomes conscious of who God really is, and when one realizes that He who is Almighty, and infinitely Holy, has done great things to us, the only possible reaction is the cry of half-articulated exultation that bursts from the depths of our being in amazement at the tremendous, inexplicable goodness of God to men and women."[85]

And so I pray, this time with more feeling,

> *Blessing and everlasting blessing,*
> *Blessing everlasting and blessing.*

The Lord Sustains Me

O LORD, how many are my foes!
  How many rise up against me!
Many are saying of me,
  "God will not deliver him."
But you are a shield around me, O LORD;
  you bestow glory on me and lift up my head.
To the LORD I cry aloud,
  and he answers me from his holy hill.
I lie down and sleep;
  I wake again, because the LORD sustains me.
I will not fear the tens of thousands
  drawn up against me on every side.
Arise O LORD!
  Deliver me, O my God!

—DAVID, THE PSALMIST

I CANNOT SAY I AM SURROUNDED BY ENEMIES the way the psalmist was, fighting for life in a pitched physical battle, in flight from his son Absalom—living in a time of *war*. My enemies seem so mundane, so innocuous in comparison.

Even so, I believe it appropriate to make Psalm 3:1–7 my own. I face forces that seem set against me. The universe does not always show a friendly face. People are not always kind; sometimes they are cruel. Some of the events in our lives seem even to come from a hand of malice: a coworker who complains about us and spreads (or starts) rumors; a family member who spews anger and hurtful words; a spouse who seems to grow vindictive or gets abusive; perhaps even a mugger or a violent neighbor. Even the most isolated and protected of us cannot escape all risk and danger. Who of us can claim never to face at least the threat of enemies? Why should I think myself an exception?

And that is not all. Apart from what others might do or not do, I need deliverance from internal stresses. Losing hope, feeling defeat, getting scared, growing confused—these states of mind may array themselves against me, nagging and troubling my soul. They hinder my walk through and toward an abundant life.

These facts of our lives, I see again this morning, have great relevance for prayer. For my own praying this week. My anxieties, I find in a lesson I must relearn—and learn again—need not become distractions keeping me from prayer, but actually become grist *for* prayer. They drive me to my knees. They make me a praying man.

It is said that someone asked Abba Macarius, an Egyptian monk in the fourth century, "How should one pray?" "No need to make long speeches," he said. "It is enough to stretch out one's hands and say, 'Lord, as you will, and as you know, have mercy.' And if the conflict grows fiercer say, 'Lord, help!' God knows very well what we need and he shows mercy."

Eugene Peterson helps me make the connection profoundly. The first motion in Psalm 3, he says, is a cry of need. He writes,

"O Lord, how many are my foes!" is thus the first sentence in the first prayer of the Psalms (3:1). Brief, urgent, frightened words—a person in trouble, crying out to God for help. The language is personal, direct, desperate. This is the language of prayer: men and women calling out their trouble—pain, guilt, doubt, despair—to God. Their lives are threatened. If they don't get help they will be dead, or diminished to some critical degree. The language of prayer is forged in the crucible of trouble.[86]

∾

I got anxious today about deciding, finally, that I would indeed go to a conference, a conference on prayer and fasting. My anxiety was not from whether I wanted to go—that was clear—but from whether I could *afford* to go—from the standpoint of both my checkbook and my date book. Yet I seemed to get a clear sense to go. Jill, too, from her own praying, came up with a "yes." So did my prayer partner and friend, Mary Lee. So I will make travel and registration arrangements today.

But still I do battle internally. In my private world exist enemies of fear, of potentially paralyzing anxiety. And there are, I believe, spiritual forces, what the apostle Paul called the "powers of this dark world and . . . the spiritual forces of evil in the heavenly realms" (Ephesians 6:12). I believe much does contend against us when we do good or turn to God.

"All that inhabits the spiritual realm," I wrote in a book on prayer some time ago, "is not pure and good. . . . For centuries spiritual writers have seen demons as more than metaphor, the devil more than symbol. . . . Evil taunts us with a seductive voice and oily reasoning. It arises within us, yet we also know it as a force outside of us. . . . We should not be alarmed when prayer requires our donning the armor of faith, or calling out to God in Jesus' name for the power of the Holy Spirit."[87]

I feel personally vulnerable right now. This whole process of discernment for ordination makes me feel scrutinized, my motives examined for flaws, my aspirations questioned. I suppose something similar happens in any job or career: a job interview for an important position or an annual performance review. Or questioning from other spheres: a family member who turns away in hurt, a colleague who betrays our trust, a church member who criticizes us, unfairly we think. Through it all, however, we learn to pray. Not just in the high and holy moments, but in the everyday ones.

And David's psalm shows me how that's done:

> *I lie down and sleep;*
> *I wake again, because the LORD sustains me.*

Drawn up on every side are enemies—thousands of them, *tens* of thousands—and yet, morning, evening, and night: I do what everyone does: I wake up, lie down, and go to sleep. *And then I wake up.* I begin again to pray God's protection upon the day to come. I wake because the Lord sustains me.

In a sense it is that simple—I lie down and go to sleep, day in and day out. And then the Lord grants me another day in which to wake up. He enables me to do it. Someday, of course, I will sleep and *not* wake up. Or perhaps awaken one day only to die before I can sleep again.

But even then I need not worry. Even when the last enemy, as the Bible calls death, overtakes me, I will not be overcome. Because I am God's. His shield covers me through life and even through the great passage into death.

Extravagant Mercies

How unworthy I am, O Lord, and sinful. But I will still bless and praise you because you have showered me with extravagant mercies.[88]

—EPHRAIM OF SYRIA, (AUTHOR'S RENDERING)

IT WAS A STARTLING REQUEST.

"Write out your sins," the speaker said. "List on a sheet of paper the sins that trouble you tonight. The sins that need the Lord's forgiveness."

The speaker at the conference on fasting and prayer, Dr. Bill Bright, wanted us to begin the conference free from the specter of guilt. By naming our wrongs, he said, we would let God rob them of their accusing power. By confessing them we would experience freedom.

The Houston hotel ballroom, packed with hundreds of attendees from around the country, almost all agreeing to fast from food as a sign of sincerity and discipline of faith, grew still. A hush spread across the room under the chandelier lighting.

And so I reflected and prayed. And I wrote. I ended up with three sins:

Anxiety.

Irritability.

Attachment to things that gratify.

And then Dr. Bright said, "Listen to this verse of scripture: 'If we confess our sins, he is faithful and just and will forgive us our sins and purify us from all unrighteousness.'" Those words from 1 John 1:9 constituted a promise, he reminded us. "Think of the sins you have named in light of that promise. And remember the forgiveness that is yours."

❀

The rest of the conference *was* significantly different because of that simple opening exercise in confession and forgiveness. I felt lighter, somehow more ready to listen and pray and fast.

To no surprise, then, I find myself, while searching for a prayer for this week, moved by the prayer of a Syrian Christian monk who lived less than three centuries after Christ. He has been called "the harp of the Holy Spirit" for his lilting poetry and lyrical hymns. He even penned his sermons in verse. And he wrote tomes on theology and Scripture. He argued persuasively for right belief at a time when heresies threatened the life of the still-young church. But what he believed never strayed far from his daily experience of prayer.

And through his prayer I have found myself moved by his experience of what moved me earlier this week, as well: his eloquent depiction of his state before God. And, all the more amazing for it, his awed gratitude for God's never-failing forgiveness.

How unworthy I am, O Lord, and sinful.

I know that my "short list" of sins doesn't begin to exhaust the ways I wander. Ways I want for myself what I should wish for others. Ways I ignore God in my pursuit of my agenda. I sometimes refuse to see what I don't want to see. And so I have to confess. I have to call out, like the blind man who heard Jesus was approaching, "Jesus, Son of David, have mercy on me!" (Luke 18:38).

∾

Ephraim, I find, is also eloquent in describing the antidote to sin, the "medicine of life," as some of the ancient writers call God's grace. For my sense of unworthiness this morning does not make me cower, but come. It makes me seek a goodness I know I don't deserve but that I nevertheless cannot do without. It fills me with praise.

And here, too, Ephraim puts into beautiful words what I might only mutter if I did not have him prompting me:

> *You have showered me with extravagant mercies.*

That is what I need! To be, as one translation puts it, "lavished" with God's mercy. What can I do or say, when met with such goodness, but to offer back words that give glory to God?

"The essence of prayer is weakness," said Eddie Smith, another of the speakers at the conference on fasting and prayer. "However, we prefer to be strong, to act as though we are in control." We don't pray more, pray enough, he said, "because we don't feel our need strongly enough. But when we know our need for mercy, it drives us to God, seeking God's favor and forgiveness."

Just as my need for mercy has this week. Just as I want it to every week. Every day. Always.

Stop, Look, and Listen

O heavenly father, who has filled the world with beauty: Open our eyes to behold your gracious hand in all your works, that, rejoicing in your whole creation, we may learn to serve you with gladness; for the sake of him through whom all things were made, your Son Jesus Christ our Lord.[89]

—THE BOOK OF COMMON PRAYER

THIS PRAYER HAS HELPED ME WHILE I'VE been running on this unseasonably warm November day. The trees are bare but silhouetted against a morning sky. It is not hard to see how God has filled the world with beauty as I trot down the hill in front of my house, on a rise overlooking a still mostly rural valley. Perhaps it's not so easy to see the evidence in Serbia or Iraq or inner city Los Angeles. Or perhaps it's easier to have to trace the workings of grace amidst such suffering. To be driven to stop, look, and listen when chaos or quake shakes the complacency we comfortably stand on.

I know that for all the good things that fill my days, I often don't see clearly enough. *Open my eyes,* I pray. I need help seeing with that deeper way of seeing, a way that pierces beneath the everyday surface of circumstances or conversations, that penetrates in a way my typical hurried glances will not touch. How can I sharpen my vision for what lies beneath my everyday surroundings?

As Avery Brooke roamed over the hillside fields and through the woods near her home as a child, she recalls, "I sensed something more, a presence, a power for which I had no explanation. What was it in the sweep of the sky, the giant outcropping of rock, the sassafras leaf in my hand? I did not know, but I felt hushed by awe and quiet joy."[90] That is more the sort of seeing I mean.

Part of it has to do not only with knowing how to look, this week's prayer tells me, but also remembering what I look *at*. The world is more than hunks of rock or pillars of lumber or masses of consumers. No, when I look out a window or stand beneath a sequoia redwood or enjoy another's company, I witness a handiwork. John Calvin, the great reformer of the sixteenth century, called the world around us a "theater of God's glory." We see what Eugene Peterson calls "the Creator's dazzling performance in putting together the elements of matter and arranging the components of the cosmos."[91] It doesn't always appear that way, not at first glance, but all that we see conveys the creative evidence of a Creator God.

Prayer helps me see it, helps me remember that this world is a meeting ground with the One who grounds and sustains and pervades all that is. So I will keep asking, as I keep running and walking.

༄

It is Thanksgiving Day. The phrase, *Open our eyes to behold your gracious hand in all your works,* comes to my lips. If only I could quit hurrying around I might see more. It is wonderful to have this oasis of quiet, here alone in the living room, before the kids get up and the preparation for the big meal begins.

I have always loved Thanksgiving, a time for family for as long as I can remember. And also because it helps me see God's hand in all of his works—my family, this neighborhood, my church, this world. But I still need corrective eye surgery. Or at least what ancient sage Clement of Alexandria called "the eternal adjustment of vision" that lets me see what blessings the world showers on me, were I but to pay more attention. Were I a bit more able to focus. I think I have what a correspondent on an Internet discussion group called "spiritual attention deficit disorder."

I'm reminded of a passage in Frederick Buechner's autobiographical work, *Now and Then*, that has long impacted me. "I discovered," he said,

> that if you really keep your eye peeled to it and your ears open, if you really pay attention to it, even such as limited and limiting life as the one I was living on Rupert Mountain opened up onto extraordinary vistas. Taking your children to school and kissing your wife good-bye. Eating lunch with a friend. Trying to do a decent day's work. Hearing the rain patter against the windows. There is no event so commonplace but that God is present within it, always hiddenly, always leaving you room to recognize him or not to recognize him, but all the more fascinatingly because of that, all the more compellingly and hauntingly."[92]

⁓

Part of that seeing happens, paradoxically, when I also learn to look without eyes that must possess or overly analyze. Thomas Merton, I read this day after Thanksgiving, talks about "renouncing the illusory reality which created things acquire when they are seen only in their relation to our own selfish interests."[93] We cannot see things *as they are,* he means, if we see them only through our own whims and wants. They will be inevitably colored by our self-absorption. Distorted.

I gain perspective on things, then, by seeing them not only in their relation to God, but also through a different stance, a gentler grasp, in their relation to *me*. That means holding lightly the wonders God displays before me on whatever road or path I happen to travel today. When I hold with a looser grip, I can, as I pray today, learn to *serve you*. Not like a child who thinks only of getting his or her own way. Not grudgingly. But with *gladness*. A gladness that comes from a gratitude that turns me toward God with thanksgiving and turns me back to the world without compulsion to grab and hold.

Only then can I begin to even think about serving God *for the sake of him through whom all things were made*. Already, with Advent around the corner, I am thinking of that Life, that Presence, that coming to the world of God's own Son. I don't want to miss the meaning of what I am about to celebrate.

Help me, O God, to stop, look, and listen.

Make Ready, Make Room

Merciful God, who sent your messengers the prophets to preach repentance and prepare the way for our salvation: Give us grace to heed their warnings and forsake our sins, that we may greet with joy the coming of Jesus Christ our Redeemer; who lives and reigns with you and the Holy Spirit, one God, now and forever. Amen.

—THE BOOK OF COMMON PRAYER

A HURRIED, HARRIED TIME AGAIN—SCRAM-bling to meet another deadline. How I long for a saner schedule. But I also feel an edge of another anticipation in the air—not just for a project completed, but for the holiday I realize soon approaches. Already our mantle decorations are out—candles and greens—already our two youngest children have set up our wintry ceramic Christmas village on the piano top, complete with wispy white cotton batting for snow.

Advent begins this week, that season leading up to Christmas observed by many Christians as a time of getting ready, waiting, hoping. *Try,* I tell myself as I do every season, *not to get too busy this time to take in, to notice, to pray.*

I also must prepare for an "Advent Quiet Day" this Saturday at a church in Virginia, followed by a sermon there the next day.

As I work and write and plan, I realize I will preach to myself. I have begun praying the prayer from *The Book of Common Prayer* that reminds me of the stern yet hopeful message of the Old Testament prophets. *Give us grace to heed their warnings and forsake our sins, that we may greet with joy the coming of Jesus Christ our Redeemer.* The Old Testament prophets preached a warning, called for repentance, pointed to who was to come.

What am I waiting for? Certainly for all the trappings of a holiday, filled with the stuff of memories for my children and Jill and me, just as I remember Christmases from my childhood. Even more, though, I wait for an encounter with the One about whom all the fuss and festivity is being made.

◌◑

With Abram off to college, I decide I will tell the congregation in Virginia about a freshman son who fulfilled his parents' worst fears. The young man spent more time fraternity partying than studying. Just before he came home for Christmas he decided to write and warn Mom and Dad about his situation. He addressed the letter to his mother, hoping to appeal to her gentler nature. "I'm failing three classes," he wrote. "Prepare Father." Mom wrote back right away: "Father prepared. Prepare yourself."

That's the message, I will say: *prepare yourself.* The same message of the prophets who looked ahead to Jesus' coming. The message I need again and again to pray becomes real in my life.

Prepare yourself is a kind of motto for Advent. *Prepare yourself* is a watchword for this season. Caught up as we sometimes get in busyness and stress and destructive habits, we know that life as we have been living it isn't what it could be. We know we need to make more room for what matters. We want to prepare to meet God, to not hold back, to give him room to come in ways perhaps we have not allowed.

Advent, which literally means coming or appearing, is all about preparation. We're preparing for one who comes. Yes, he has already come. And he will come again at the end of time, to right what is wrong, to establish his kingdom in fullness. But in another sense he is right now waiting to come into our daily lives.

Our times are different from Isaiah's or John the Baptist's. We are not going out to a wilderness to hear a prophet preaching. But we have the same longing, the same spiritual hunger as their people did. We don't want to miss he who can fill us and the world with his glorious presence. . . . We want a holiday with the holy in it. Running through our Christmas preparations is an ache for nothing less than the presence of God. And so we turn our hearts toward the coming of this One who holds our only real hope. Who holds us. We say it to one another, to ourselves, over and over again: prepare yourselves. Make ready. Make room.

The preacher preaches to himself. And so I pray for a ready heart. *Give us grace to heed.*

ॐ

My New Zealand friend, best man at my wedding some twenty years ago, sent me an e-mail greeting with words of an ancient Christian writer, Isaac of Stella, a twelfth-century monk.

> May the son of God who is already formed in you, grow in you
> so that for you he will become immeasurable, and that in you
> he will become laughter, exaltation, the fullness of joy which no
> one will take from you.

It is a blessing I need. "The Word became flesh and lived among us," declares the Gospel of John. Christ *lives and reigns,* my prayer reminds me. I realize how I need Christ to come and live through the Holy Spirit amid the scenes of my life. I want to follow him. But first I must make ready to welcome him. I must make room. *Today.*

When God Shows Up

May Christ, who by his Incarnation gathered into one things earthly and heavenly, fill you with his joy and peace; and the blessing of God Almighty, the Father, the Son, and the Holy Spirit, be among you, and remain with you always. Amen.[94]
—EPISCOPAL BLESSING

NOT OFTEN DOES AN INSIGHT STRIKE ME while I stand in front of a group of people talking. I am more prone to gather my thoughts before I stand, committing them to well-ordered speaking notes.

In the traditional, neo-Gothic church in Virginia where I was speaking over the weekend, I emphasized how we practice the presence of God in small, daily ways. As I talked about Christ, whose birth we look toward on Advent Sunday, I mentioned the words of the blessing I'll be using as my prayer this week. I wanted to stress how I try to watch for traces of God in my everyday life. Of course, I admitted, I don't manage it every day. I get sucked into the vortex of urgent faxes and the need to pay the bills like anyone else. I easily get overcommitted. But this Advent, I said, I've been trying to make room for Christ and the things of Christ.

The difference, I said, comes from the promise that God will show up. That God draws near. *May Christ, who by his Incarnation gathered into one things earthly and heavenly, fill you with his joy and peace.* "May Christ," I continued, "who came, God in the flesh, walking a world of hot dusty roads and cranky employers, a world of joy and longing, pain and glory, *continue* to come."

And then it hit me anew: how Christ's appearing, his Incarnation, as the theologians call it, brought together the two worlds. So often we think of spirituality as heavenly, our jobs and household chores and childcare needs as earthly. But Christ, by becoming a *Person,* I realized, reminds us of just how these matters can be caught up into God's kingdom purposes. It happened back then; it happens today.

Now there can be no huge split between the daily and the eternal, the physical and the spiritual. Mystery finds a home in our midst. By coming, the Christ incarnated into our world of flesh and blood and broken bodies and hungry children tells us that he comes right where we are. The Son of God comes as the son of Mary and the carpenter. The high and lofty One shows up as the kid next door. He reaches out with real hands. He cries. He dies and lives again.

Amid my hurriedness I need an Advent. I need to hear a blessing. I want to let Christ come—smack in my grungy and glorious ordinariness. So I will keep praying this week that Christ—when he shows up in ways small and large, in half-noticed reminders of his love or in a quiet, subtle presence—will bring joy and peace. If I am not too busy, I will know it. The Father, Son, and Holy Spirit, as far beyond my normal range of vision as they are, will become part of my walking and waking, my working and waiting.

Follow the Light

My dearest Lord,
Be Thou a bright flame before me,
Be Thou a guiding star above me,
Be Thou a smooth path beneath me,
Be Thou a kindly shepherd behind me,
Today and evermore.[95]

—COLUMBA

I SHIFTED UNCOMFORTABLY AS I SAT ON THE folding chair in his office. "I'm unconvinced," Tom had said, in so many words. "Why do you think you should pursue ordination?"

I was not expecting such a grilling. Not considering the fruit my work over the years has seemed to bear. But my friend Tom, a local pastor eager to advise me, hesitated to confirm the calling I believe has re-emerged. Ordination to ministry means service to a church, he stressed. Was my wanting to keep writing and leading retreats a legitimate expression of a pastor's call? Was I aspiring to be ordained in a new denominational home for how it would aid my ministry, give me more contacts for workshops? Had I entered this exploration process without concern for my "own" ministry?

I found my face flushing with discomfort and irritation.

I understood Tom's line of reasoning. Ordination in the

Episcopal Church *would* mean understandings of church and calling different than from those of the Church of the Brethren, where I had served as pastor before. And I know myself well enough to understand how mixed even my loftier motivations can be. The desire to serve Christ sometimes mingles with my selfish ambitions.

So I will continue to search my soul.

But I will also recall yet again how living by calling versus career means resolutely attending to the ways *God* leads. Taking sanctified risks. Watching for confirmation through open doors. Like a beach ball I may try to submerge in ocean waters, a call keeps resurfacing. It will not go easily away. I don't want to be hard-headed, but I must also follow where I think God is taking me.

And so, as in so many situations, I find myself thrown back to God in prayer. Driven to seek guidance.

∾

Over the years I have experienced critical moments of guidance. One Sunday afternoon while I was in high school, settling on my college choices, reflecting on a Sunday school class I had just attended, I sensed a simple, sure awareness that I should become a minister. I began to *know.* I did not tell anyone at first, and let the divine nudge grow stronger; and then, as I shared tentatively at first, I let those I trusted in on what I thought. The path seemed clear.

Then, years later, having been a pastor already for six years, there was the crisp November night I took a walk under the stars in our suburban Houston neighborhood. Coming with an intensity that would have astonished me a decade earlier, I felt with dawning certainty that my growing interest in writing was "right." "I felt something deep in me relax," I later wrote in my journal, "and say yes." There was no audible voice, but some deep part of me knew what I was to be about. I would eventually devote several years to editing and writing full-time for religious publishers.

But all is not settled. Now a reemerging call to pastor seems to beckon me to a converging of the two roads. I have never really discarded the pastoral dimension of my vocation. Now where will it take me? *Show me* your *way, O Lord!*

⟡

Last night Jill and I attended a meeting of candidates for ordination of our Episcopal diocese—a Christmas party at the bishop's home with members of the diocesan commission on ministry. Everyone in attendance was aware that the diocese could receive only so many new ministry candidates. There were more aspirants than available slots. For all the festive atmosphere, most of us seemed guarded. Later we introduced ourselves around the circle, men and women from churches all around the diocese. And the bishop spoke, stressing how ministry requires being willing to go wherever sent.

Jill and I talked in the car on the way home from the party, both of us reflective. When I shared my struggle over giving up some of my freedom and autonomy, Jill, with her own aspirations to ministry, asked me: "Are you willing to trust God to work out his will throughout this process? Are you willing to let go of 'your' career?"

⟡

So I pray this morning, *Be Thou a bright flame before me.* How I need that light on the way! And the warmth that fire brings—the way it overcomes cold uncertainties and fears. All this I need—and not just for my vocational issues, but for all of life. "For you were once darkness," I read in the New Testament, "but now you are light in the Lord. Live as children of light" (Ephesians 5:8).

How much light will I receive today? I cannot say. How long will my discernment process last? Who can predict? It is like walking toward home on a dark night. You keep walking as far as your flashlight allows. But as you keep walking, the edge of light moves ahead. You walk to the edge of the light and eventually, step by step, find yourself where you need to be.

So I will follow the light I have. The Light within me and around me. It will get me where I need to go.

∾

Light is so much a part of this season, I think. Some of us deck our house eaves with little lights. We crowd a coffee table with candles. We line our sidewalks with luminaries. We reach out, I believe, for the reassurance that we will not sit long in darkness. How much the world around us longs for light! It recognizes it only vaguely—this Christmas season when it strives after what it does not know, after One whom it only vaguely names or understands. But the longing is there. Hopeful.

Be Thou a guiding star above me. I have been praying this, too, even before coming to this time that anticipates a star guiding the wise men to Jesus. That was a once-in-a-world occurrence, of course. But I remember how often I have preached that God does not leave us directionless. He is not stingy with his will. I need to live confidently with that conviction today.

Be Thou a smooth path beneath me. This is not, I realize, a prayer suggesting I should expect an easy life. "Unless there is an element of risk in our exploits for God," said missionary pioneer Hudson Taylor, "there is no need for faith." Whose road avoids at least occasional ups and downs, curves and corners? But I *can* pray that no obstacles will keep me from my goal. That no boulders will block my road. That when the road takes an abrupt upward rise, I will not let fatigue keep me from carrying on.

"Morgan's Steep" is the name of a rugged set of mountains and trails in a town not far from here. Steep indeed. But not untraversable. All that is needed is a little more wind. A bit more patience. A goal that draws me onward.

∽

Another day. *Be Thou a kindly shepherd behind me.* I usually think of a sheep herder going ahead, blazing the trail. But no, as Celtic sheep farmers would know well, the flock needs attention from the back, as well.

As a personality type, I look forward more than backward (and sometimes occupy the future more than the present!). But sometimes I need someone to bring up the rear. I need a shepherd behind me. Not only to prod me along, but to take care of what is left in my wake. I need a God who will deal mercifully with what I've left undone, graciously with the regrets that settle on me occasionally. I need to know that the loose ends I let go of in favor of the next urgent task will not derail what is to come, that the light I live by will not sputter out.

And so I keep praying this week, convinced that God is leading. Such convictions let me trust—at least for moments at a time. But I also know that just as Advent majors on waiting, making ready, so much of what I strike out for will ask of me patience. I won't be able to get by, much less reach my destination or fulfill my calling, unless God goes, as the Celtic prayer has it, before, above, beneath, and behind—surrounding, in other words, all my days.

God with Us

O Come, Desire of nations bind
All peoples in one heart and mind
From Dust that brought us forth to life;
Deliver us from earthly strife.
Rejoice! Rejoice!
Emmanuel shall come to thee, O Israel.
—LATIN HYMN

ALREADY THIS HAS BEEN A WEEK WITH plenty of longing, even apart from its being a season of waiting and watching. I've had little trouble remembering to ask God to come, as this Advent hymn from the ninth century implores—into my life, into this world. It has been a week of strife, into which I know I must invite the One who comes to bind together and fulfill. I need Emmanuel—"God with us" the name means—to be *here*.

Last night Jill said she felt discouraged about a tension that crops up between us sometimes, a relationship pattern that causes both of us hurt. "Sometimes I feel it's hopeless," she said with a mixture of sadness and irritation. "It seems like there is no way for us ever to completely break the cycle."

We both know well what happens: When I feel under stress, my need for Jill's presence and attention grows stronger. I reach out, sometimes intensely. When Jill feels under pressure from work, on the other hand, she tends to withdraw, to need "space." Which of course only heightens my neediness, and escalates her emotional distancing. What an ugly cycle that creates! Sometimes even when we articulate to one another what is happening, we still accuse and lash out. For all our profound love and compatibility, the hard feelings run deep.

We have learned, however, that no matter how tension rises between us, prayer can help us break the downward spiral. We turn our eyes, at least for a moment, off of the one we argue with to One we know loves us both. We are careful not to use our words of prayer as barbs, but as an honest crying out. The tension doesn't magically dissolve, but the shift in our sight is often all that is needed for another pattern, a wave of grace, to come washing in onto the shore of our hearts.

∞

The hymn I am praying this week reminds me of other, deeper strifes: the recent days of bombing Iraq, just concluded. Our nation divided by an unpopular impeachment of a leader who has admitted to failing his nation. When I see such agitation and dissension I know that the world needs more than ingenuity. It needs the presence of the One who made us and still sustains us. My longing turns into prayer.

> *O Come, Desire of nations bind*
> *All peoples in one heart and mind*
> *From Dust that brought us forth to life;*
> *Deliver us from earthly strife.*

How we live amid incompleteness, I think, *amid circumstances that leave us waiting for answers, for deliverance.* Recently I read about an Episcopal bishop in Sudan who was imprisoned, who witnessed horrible suffering and persecution among his people. His prayer, his constant refrain, was stark and direct: "Lord, come!" *Maranatha,* he prayed, just as the early church uttered the prayer in the Aramaic language in the fires of persecution.

The longing confronts me weekly as I attend church with our local Sudanese refugees who have fled horrible suffering. I think about these things—not often enough, not so much that I feel driven to help as I might. But hearing of such suffering does prompt me and compel me to invite Emmanuel—literally "God with us"—to continue to rule over a broken world. Jesus, whose coming we anticipate and celebrate this season, *is* Emmanuel. I pray, as I prayed the week I used the Lord's Prayer, *Your kingdom come.* How we all need a visitation.

∾

One of the books on my shelves is entitled *Yearning,* written by a pastor and fellow alumnus of Princeton Seminary, Craig Barnes. The book's subtitle reminds me of how much longing will be a part of our lives: *Living Between How It Is and How It Ought to Be.*

"Hope," Barnes writes, "is no unrealistic refusal to look squarely at life's horrors." No, he writes, hope "arises out of the hard truth of how things are. Christians will always live carrying in one hand the promises of how it will be and in the other the hard reality of how it is. To deny either is to hold only half the truth of the gospel."[96]

This past Sunday at church as we sang "O Come, O Come," the Sudanese, many still in their twenties and thirties, sang as well, singing with what I imagine is a pathos most of us in our suburban comforts will not touch. But we all linked our voices. I sing with believers the world over, it turns out, to put longing to melody, to take pain and transmute it through music into expectant worship. *O God, who took dust and breathed in life in that primordial story of origins, breathe life still into my life, our home, the world.*

❧

It is Christmas Eve. Last night we observed Advent as a family, in our living room. We have a three-foot felt wall hanging cut into a Christmas tree, adorning the wall. Each evening we read from a booklet a verse or two, say a printed prayer, and pull out of a pouch yet another symbolic felt ornament.

Bekah likes the concreteness of the devotion—something she can feel, touch, handle. Each felt piece represents a person or idea meaningful in Christian faith—a heart, angel, lamb, shoot from the stump of Jesse (Isaiah 11:1–3). Last night the ornament-symbol depicted gold, frankincense, and myrrh, the gifts the wise men would bring to the baby Jesus. These were admittedly difficult to picture with a felt shape, but certainly one of the three blobs, with its gold color, was easy enough to recognize.

We put the ornament on, and then said the words of this Advent hymn. We joined voices, perhaps not always fully aware of all we were asking. But our longing found words.

The Desire of the Nations! That is you, Lord Jesus. Our hope. *The Desire of me,* when I don't forget to remember who I am, what I am here for.

Being able to pray is ultimately an act of confidence. I know that this week. To dress words on our requests and longings reminds me of what can be. Of what God ultimately intends.

Hope, Lewis Smedes writes, has to do with precisely such longings. It is to not settle for the way things appear. To hope is "to see *beyond* what is to what can be. Or to see *within* what seems to be to what *really* is. This is imagination. There can be no hope without it. . . . The link between imagination and hope is broken if we think that imagination is only for such things as fables, fantasies, and fairy tales. . . . [I]maging things is also a way of seeing the most real things of all, things for which we need lenses in our souls as well as in our heads."[97]

Help us see, O Lord, how you wish to come. Here. Now. Reward our longings, that we may experience the life you bring to all who turn to you.

The Clear Light of Day

*Thy light, O Jesus the Lord, has shone out over all creation
and scattered the darkness of error. May thy light shine now
in our souls also, O Jesus our King Who art the true light.*[98]
—SAINT EPHRAIM THE SYRIAN

I WRITE ON CHRISTMAS EVE, EARLY, BEFORE
the house has stirred, already having prayed for several days
the simple prayer of this fourth-century Christian (also spelled
Ephraem, whose prayer I used an earlier week). I have been praying
for Jesus' *light to shine in our souls, to scatter the works of darkness.*

What does it mean to pray this way? From my earliest memories of hearing and reading the Bible, I know that to think or
speak of light is to remind myself of the goodness of God.
According to Genesis, the earth was "formless and empty" and
darkness reigned before God created light (Genesis 1:2).
Darkness meant evil, affliction, absence, even death. But God
made the day and found it "good" (Genesis 1:4). Throughout the
Bible, light symbolizes God's presence and activity. The symbols
that shine from the candles adorning our dining room and blink-
ing on our Christmas tree, for all their inviting warmth, become
pale reflections of the true Light. For in the Bible light becomes
a figure for what saves us: God's Word is called a lamp that guides
us or a light that enlightens us. God himself is called "my light

and my salvation" (Psalm 27:1). And there is Jesus, coming in opposition to all darkness, declaring, "I am the light of the world. Whoever follows me will never walk in darkness, but will have the light of life" (John 8:12). No wonder I find myself drawn to praying to one whose light *shone out over all creation.*

Ephraim, too, I will discover, understood the vivid reality of the words *darkness* and *light.* He lived in awe of the babe Jesus born in an unlit stable, yet coming as light. And he knew how desperately the world lives under the domination of darkness, a darkness that had to be scattered not by an occasional word of illumination but by an incarnation of God's radiance.

For a time Ephraim preached at "street level," concerned to share his faith in Christ with harlots and heretics alike. When aberrant teaching arose in the church, he closeted himself away in a study to write books to defend the truth and rightly expound the scriptures. During one period he spent much of his time evangelizing pagans, but then he felt called to the rigors of the solitary ascetic. Still, he would use his voice and his pen in ways that sometimes astonished his listeners or readers. Ephraim worked tirelessly, eloquently, to communicate the glimmers of light that so captivated him and so lit up his poetry and fueled his preaching.

Once a prostitute tried to entice him to sin, if only, she thought, to rile his anger, for he had a reputation for even temperedness.

"Come with me," he said to her when she approached him on the road. She followed while he led her to a crowded place, milling with people.

"Let us lie down here and commit fornication together," he said.

She was appalled. "How could we stop here, with so many people around? Wouldn't we be ashamed?

"If you are ashamed before the people, how much more ashamed should you feel before God?"

At that the woman left in shame, "able neither," says one biographer, "to seduce the saint into sin, nor to incite him to anger, for he was truly a man without guile, meek and utterly incapable of wrath."[99]

◌

I think of the darkness near me. The things that cause me concern. The places in our world where light is desperately needed. It has not been hard, this season, to think of them. The winter holds fears of cold for the homeless. Darkness falls literally on the hundreds of thousands in Eastern Tennessee and Virginia who have been without electricity for days on end from ice storms and downed power lines. And I think of air attacks and skirmishes with Iraq, the dark prospect of weapons of mass destruction.

And I think of the darkness from which some reach out for hope this season, yet not knowing or really wanting to know where it is to be found, with *whom* it is to be found. I remember friends and family members who wander without the Light.

And I see darkness in myself—fears about my vocational questions, tension in my relationship with Jill that sometimes darkens my mood. Sometimes—too often—I don't see things in the clear light of day. The sleepy after-effects of spiritual slumber make me miss seeing things. Just as at night, stumbling in the dark on my way to answer a late phone call, I might stub my toe or find my mind foggy, so I need the bracing effects of day. I need light in my soul. My eyes long for at least the promise of morning.

Ephraim's little prayer helps. It shakes up my sleepy soul. It reminds me of the light of Christ flooding the world already.

And now, not quite 8:00 A.M., sitting comfortably in the living room, the sun begins to stream into the window to my right.

It shines so stunningly bright it makes it hard for me to see well enough to keep writing.

And so, as the sun chases away the unconsciousness of sleep and sometimes uneasy dreams, as the light reminds me of the beauty of another day, I recall how Jesus came to obliterate the error and darkness of night. Our world needs light to flood all of life as we know it. *Lord, how I need light.*

The true light. Your light.

A Holy Letting Go

*Lord, you know what I want and, if it is your will, whether
I should have it. And if it is not your will, good Lord, do not
be displeased, for I want only what you want.*[100]
—JULIAN OF NORWICH

ON THIS FIRST DAY OF JANUARY, GROGGY
from staying up to mark a holiday, I think of the year just
passed, inventorying what I have gotten done, what dreams went
unfulfilled. But even more, my thoughts turn to the year to
come. While I long ago gave up listing resolutions, I still can't
resist trying to peek ahead to what another year will bring. I grow
reflective—and curious.

With the household about to stir awake, and New Year's Day
visiting to be done, I barely manage to copy the prayer of Julian
into my journal. I had run across it in my reading days before,
and the tie-in to today struck me as obvious. I can begin the year
with at least a few moments with it. I decide it makes a good way
to start anew.

෨෧

I'm back at my praying, January 2. This morning, as I pray, so
many things I could ask for still crowd my mind: success for the

book that comes out early this year, acceptance into the ordination process, money for Abram's college and for needed improvements on our house. I can think endlessly of what I would like! And I turn them into requests before God.

But Julian's prayer helps me quiet the nagging neediness. *Lord,* I ask, *are these wishes what you want me to ask for—want me to have at all?*

As I have discovered already, Julian lived in a dark time in English history. The plague of Black Death and the grinding bloodshed of the Hundred Years' War would have sobered anyone. And there was famine, and the violence of the Peasants' Revolt, which the ruling class cruelly repressed. The local peasant leader, Geoffrey Litser, was executed near Julian's cell inside the church where she lived. Julian nevertheless went about her praying with a compelling sense of the love of God and the love of the crucified Christ. So compelled was she to grow closer to God that she even asked, in a sentiment foreign indeed to our times, for suffering, believing it would bring her closer to God. And she asked for a huge longing for God, and to have God satisfy that appetite. All that lies behind this prayer, which she explains in some detail in her book, *Revelations.*

But she also knew the likely shortsightedness of any prayer, even one that on the surface might seem the ultimate in piousness or selflessness. And so, after asking God to allow her to be purified through suffering, she admitted, "I knew this was not the common way of prayer."[101] Perhaps, she realized, she was getting too involved in trying to figure out God's means to make her what he intended. So she prays instead these words of letting go. They speak to me in a way perhaps different from what she meant, but they nevertheless stretch me.

And so I consider all my wants and longings, usually far less noble than Julian's, and likewise seek from God a holy lack of inordinate attachment. I realize my need to, as Richard Foster once put it, resign as CEO of my little universe. I want to be free of my incessant need to orchestrate. I realize that means giving up some control, and in a world that sometimes seems chaotic, that prospect can be unsettling indeed. But at the beginning of each morning—each year—I choose to watch for what God is already about. I open my clenched fingers to place the details into Hands larger than my own. I leave room for divine accidents. I give the day into God's capable care.

I do not easily let go of things I habitually grasp; nor, I suspect, do any of us eagerly admit our insufficiency. But the way Julian leads me to pray means forfeiting a compulsive need to achieve or accomplish. And when I do let go, I make room for the Lord's sovereign work.

"In returning and rest you shall be saved; in quietness and in trust shall be your strength," the Old Testament prophet declared (Isaiah 30:15, NRSV). Slowly I become willing to live another way, a way that allows for space to pray, to invite God in, instead of my always charging in.

Can I do that consistently and profoundly? This morning, looking at experience from years past, I know I cannot on my own. And so I pray, *It is only in you and with you, O Lord, that I find the grace and wherewithal to even hope that could happen. Please Lord, help me to get to the place where I say, "I want only what you want."*

⁓

What will the new year hold? I am curious and occasionally anxious. But ultimately I look forward with deep hope and anticipation. Why? As it happens in so many movements in the spiritual life, trust makes possible unheard-of, undreamed realities, hidden in the everyday world I walk through this morning, tomorrow, and however long I have to live.

For some time I have been struck by a little book by a French writer from an earlier century named Jean-Pierre de Caussade. "There is never," he said,

> a moment when God does not come forward in the guise of some suffering or some duty, and all that takes place with us, around us and through us both includes and hides his activity. Yet, because it is invisible, we are always taken by surprise and do not recognize his operation until it has passed us by. If we could lift the veil and if we watched in vigilant attention, God would endlessly reveal himself to us and we should see and rejoice in his active presence in all that befalls us. At every moment we should exclaim, "It is the Lord!" (John 21:7).[102]

I hope, as this first week of a new year begins, to carry into it more of that kind of spirit. I don't want God to be displeased with what I ask. But if I ask according to his will, if I pray, like Jesus, *your* will be done, chances are I can't go too far wrong.

Focusing on God

Through humility you will show me what I am, what I have been, and from whence I came, for I am nothing, and did not know. If I am left to myself, then I am nothing and all is frailty and imperfection; but if you vouchsafe a little regard to me, soon I am made strong and filled with a new joy. . . . I have lost you, and myself as well, by the inordinate love I have had for myself; in seeking you again I have found both you and myself. Therefore, I will from now on more deeply set myself at naught and more diligently seek you than I have done in times past.[103]

—THOMAS À KEMPIS

MY DEFENSES ARE UP. AN EVALUATOR FOR my ordination discernment process just wrote unflattering comments. I don't know if she intended for me to see them or not, but the force of her words stunned me. Even my motives were questioned. I believe, as do others I know I can trust, that my nemesis did not know me well. She has misunderstood some things. So I tell myself.

But the issue goes deeper, I know. I am *not* perfect. And why expect always to be liked and applauded, still less always warmly patted? Yet that is somehow my underlying assumption and expectation. *Of course* everyone is going to approve of me. *Of course* I should never expect criticism. After all, I'm a nice guy.

And so my mind runs overtime, fixating on the criticism. No matter that all the other evaluations have been glowing. I have trouble shaking the one that wasn't.

Such is the state of my mind as I come across Thomas à Kempis's words, found, once again, in the dog-eared book I read years ago, *The Imitation of Christ*. I highlighted the passage, certainly not knowing then how much it might speak to me later—now. While I find my self-justifications wildly at work, while I find myself unsettled and angry, à Kempis seems to say, "No need to get upset." *Even if the worst of my evaluator's comments fit*, I tell myself, *I would still be in the same place: in great need of divine mercy and strength*. And the words remind me to ask myself, *What am I to take from this humbling experience? Can God help me grow through this?* How could he not?

For one, Thomas's difficult words pierce through my self-absorption: *Through humility you will show me what I am, what I have been, and from whence I came, for I am nothing, and did not know*. For all their icy austerity, such words massage the soul in necessary ways. Thomas overstates, I believe; God did not make *nothing*. God made *us*. And we *are* something. Humankind is the crown of creation. Of his chosen people he says, "they [are] . . . like the jewels in a crown" (Zechariah 9:16). But how our petty prides—how *my* little preoccupations—need puncturing! Next to the greatness of God our pet schemes and (we think) impressive achievements are dwarfed indeed. Thomas is a tonic for our silly smallness and insistence that the world turn around us.

With all that settled, you'd think I could easily think, *How much can it matter—really—that someone has concluded I have some deficiencies?* But it is not so simple, partly because the issue goes much deeper. We are not who we are because we are so wonderful, or even "okay," as pop psychology of an earlier decade emphasized. No, we owe whatever we are to the reality (often forgotten) that God lovingly embraces us, invites us close, puts up with us daily. God makes us who we are and inspires us to become more than the little we are. *If I am left to myself, then I am nothing and all is frailty and imperfection.* Paul the apostle said not, "I can do it all," but rather, "I can do all things through him who strengthens me" (Philippians 4:13, NRSV).

Though we sometimes think that what we really want is to be left alone, *left to myself* becomes a hardship. Solitary confinement is one of our severest sentences. My protective instincts—my "inordinate love for myself" as Thomas calls it—actually walls me off from the Source of what matters, what makes life rich.

But with God, the outlook shifts dramatically. *If you vouchsafe a little regard to me, soon I am made strong and filled with a new joy.* Bill Griffin, my friend working on a fresh rendering of *The Imitation* into contemporary English, translates these words like this: "If, however, you take even a quick look at me, a sidelong glance maybe, I take on new strength, new joy." That is what I will attempt to do: Stop obsessing about myself and try to remember God's regard for me, in spite of my weaknesses and pride. *What could possibly matter more?*

ॐ

And that is what will make the difference, indeed, on another day. In my reading I again come across this statement from the philosopher Soren Kierkegaard: "Purity of heart is to will one thing."[104] Jesus said it best: "Seek first his kingdom and his righteousness" (Matthew 6:33).

So even while I react defensively, I pray. And that act of devotion helps remind me that perhaps I should pay attention to any truth contained in criticism aimed my direction. I need humility (to come properly, humbly to God) and yet also discernment (to keep me from being inordinately discouraged). The way between those means comes through what Thomas and John of the Cross emphasize—focus on God.

I have long been struck by how that recognition stole upon one man, traveling in Europe:

> I entered the cathedral at Gloucester on a tour. Circumstances were hardly conducive to a religious experience. We had forty-five minutes off the bus. A crowd of tourists was around; the cathedral itself was not spectacular, particularly in comparison to many others. So it was completely by surprise that I was swept away.
>
> I was standing alone in the nave, looking at the vaulted ceiling. The organist had come in to practice, and was playing. The music shifted. One strong, clear bass note sounded. Around that one note the melody swirled. I found that within me, something was bowed to the ground on the steadiness of that note. It called me, brought by soul to its knees, then lifted me up. I . . . knew what it was to be brought low and then lifted up; to be a creature in the presence of something high.[105]

∞

Another day begins. I find myself filled with a new joy as I try to let criticism be an occasion for going deeper. In choosing to focus on God instead of myself, my appearances, my little defense mechanisms, I learn again the paradox of finding myself by losing myself. *Therefore, I will from now on more deeply set myself at naught and more diligently seek you than I have done in times past.*

At least that is how Thomas helps me pray. It may not hold for long, but at least for now it gives me the grace of a glimpse of another way. And that will hold me until another day.

An Infusing Presence

Almighty God, look upon my life and cause all darkness and doubt to vanish beneath your gaze. Look upon my ministry and banish all barriers to effectiveness and faithfulness. Fill my life and ministry with your Holy Spirit to the end that I may be led this day into paths of fruitful service. Amen.[106]
—RUEBEN JOB AND NORMAN SHAWCHUCK

EVERY NOW AND THEN I GET A GLIMPSE OF another way to live, of another source of energy for all the responsibilities I face—as a father, a husband, a writer, a church member, a *person*. Not quite a drastic, cataclysmic shift in perspective, but a glimpse. Even that makes a difference.

Today gave me such a moment of seeing, smack in the midst of my hurrying around. I was making final preparations for a men's retreat I'm to lead for a local church. I was packing, making sure the kids had done the lunch dishes, gathering all my notes and overhead transparencies. Just before I got in the car to drive the ninety interstate minutes to the conference center, I remembered I needed a prayer for this week. Out of the corner of my eye I caught sight of *A Guide to Prayer for Ministers and Other Servants,* compiled by Rueben Job, a retired and wise Methodist bishop, and Norman Shawchuck.

Thumbing through the book I saw a prayer I instantly realized aptly framed my need. For how I tend to make every project a solo endeavor! I strive and sigh and pull hard. I think everything that happens depends on me, on my getting it right, on my figuring out the best approach or line of attack.

I think of my parenting. I pray for my children and ask for guidance as I raise them, but how often, in the midst of the daily routine—making sure they do their school work, keeping them from fighting, teaching them right from wrong—do I operate as though everything depends on *me*. I try endlessly to manage, sometimes even manipulate. I so often forget to pray my way through the day's demands and opportunities. I tend not to let things unfold without all my "help."

I think about the retreat I'm about to lead, with the theme, "God as My Anchor." There is irony here! I too easily approach every presentation, every article, even ordinary conversations with a performance mentality. *Will I be witty enough?* I fret. *Poised? Appropriately outgoing?* I even turn a spiritual life retreat into an occasion to worry about whether or not I will be entertaining! But amid the preparations—all my searching for just the right story or punchline, all my careful scheduling of the event—I desperately need to invite Another into the process. I need to anchor my life fully in God.

And so into the mix of my anxieties comes a subtle turn—away from the clamoring demands and toward a calming Presence. I find something in beginning to settle down.

∽

As I finish packing, my last-minute jitters make me both more frantic and more convinced I need the help of One to whom I can say, *look upon my life and cause all darkness and doubt to vanish beneath your gaze.* If God does not show up, my best thoughts will not truly transform a life. Without his light my little sparks of insight will never ignite a soul. Without his profound personal presence my halting pointing will not fill another with faith. When I stop to think about it, I realize, how can I expect to do anything worthwhile *without* God's blessing, help, and presence?

And that is precisely the prayer I need. Given how I tend to want things "just so," given how I tend to organize and orchestrate minute details, I constantly need to be pulled back from my occupations and obsessions. *Fill my life and ministry with your Holy Spirit,* I pray. "Know," says a psalm,

> that the LORD is God.
> It is he that made us, and we are his;
> we are his people, and the sheep of his pasture
> (Psalm 100:3).

There is a variant reading, my Bible's footnote tells me, depending on which ancient manuscripts one consults. The psalm could also read, "It is he that made us, and *not we ourselves.*" I like that rendering, too. I haven't made myself and I won't make or break this retreat. What happens will hinge on more profound matters, a more certain Presence.

I take a moment to copy down my prayer to take along on the trip. I cannot hope to succeed this weekend if I forget to seek God's transforming power.

෨෬

I'm on the interstate, running a few minutes behind, the anxiety mounting again, and I remember that just before leaving I had put the index card with the prayer scrawled on it in my pocket.

As the typical last-minute worries about the final details surface, I glance at a phrase. Especially, *Look upon my ministry and banish all barriers to effectiveness and faithfulness.* I tell myself, *God will take care of the barriers. God will help me say what needs to be said.*

I think of all the ways in which people minister—as teachers, administrators, plumbers, child caregivers. I will be addressing some sixty men at the retreat. I already know some of their stories. They come from varied backgrounds—young and old, single and married, childless and blessed with multiple grandchildren. They go to very different workplaces. Some no longer work at all. But I want to help them think of their jobs and activities as opportunities. Not just to earn money or fill time, but to live out a calling. I want them to invite God to banish all barriers to being more than they have been in all the settings of their lives. And that movement begins right now, with me, even as I sit patiently behind a traffic tie-up on the interstate onramp.

∽

My mentor in this area has been the late Henri Nouwen, who I read as a young pastor. I should say I turned to him *desperately* when I began to realize my own personal store of inspiration and insight was not going to instill my ministry with profundity. He helped me realize that my self-imagined noble sermons and winning ways would not save the day. I began to see how relying on my own steam as a husband and father would soon leave me without propulsion and motivation. He wrote of leaders and workers and ministers who "have many projects, plans, and appointments, but who have lost their heart somewhere in the midst of their activities."[107] He helped me embrace the fact that in *any* area of life I need resources far beyond my own.

I saw myself in his words then, and I realize the danger now. So I take time to pray, even before things get rolling this weekend. *How can I leave more room for God?* I think about the first session about to begin with the men this evening. Instead of worrying only about doing a "good job," can I instead be concerned about whether the men will grow closer to God? Instead of an inward descending spiral, I want to walk on what my prayer this week calls *paths of service—paths of fruitful service.*

And once I get back from the retreat, turning attention again to my family and my writing, can I keep from forgetting to ask God in? Can I think more about people around me—whether I am at home or church, in a neighborhood conversation or evening Bible study, or even just sitting with a friend or stranger?

Only the Presence of Another, filling all I attempt and infusing even what I fail to do, can make that kind of difference.

The Gift of a New Day

We give you hearty thanks, O God, for the rest of the past night and for the gift of a new day with its opportunities of pleasing you. Grant that we so pass its hours in the perfect freedom of your service, that at eventide we may again give thanks to you, through Jesus Christ our Lord. Amen.[108]

—EASTERN ORTHODOX PRAYER

THIS MORNING, LATE IN JANUARY, I FIND myself thankful. I awakened that way. It has partly to do, I'm sure, with my healing from a terrible head cold. Coughing and fever and achiness had dulled my senses, to say nothing of the potent cold medicine. But as I get up in the dark before the sun has quite come up, as I flip on the living room lamp, the warm yellow cast on the furniture seems to glow in more ways than one. I am feeling better and am coming awake to the small wonders of the day.

This prayer helps me articulate what I experience. It reminds me to remember the incomprehensible blessings—like the gift of life itself, the opportunity of a new day. That sounds so simple on my lips. Seems so elementary. But too often, I find morning a time to rehearse the concerns of the day. I don't grapple with anxiety quite as writer Kathleen Norris describes, but I understand what she means:

For years, early morning was a time I dreaded. In the process of waking up, my mind would run with panic. All the worries of the previous day would still be with me, spinning around with old regrets as well as fears for the future. I don't know how or when the change came, but now when I emerge from night, it is with more hope than fear. I try to get outside as early as possible so that I can look for signs of first light, the faint, muddy red of dawn.[109]

But in these young hours of a day about to unfold I pray with thanksgiving, as my prayer has it, *for the rest of the past night and for the gift of a new day with its opportunities of pleasing you.* I decide that I need to shut off the worries or fantasies that play in my mind as I stir awake, and fill my heart instead with awareness of the gifts, large and small, of everyday life. I need, out of such gratitude, to think about ways I can please God.

Recently I saw above the desk of someone processing paperwork for me a little sign that said, "No whining." Did she intend it for sour, cranky customers? Perhaps, but my hunch is she put it there as much as anything to remind *herself* how to carry on through the day. I need similar reminders.

But for me, the problem is more subtle than resolving not to complain. It is not so much irritable grousing I fight. It's the way I let my daily routine drown out impulses of thankfulness. I sometimes go through life on a kind of automatic pilot, not really noticing much.

I remember how novelist and minister Frederick Buechner once told of driving through a town not far from his home. Should you have seen me, he said, you would have said that I did pass you along the road. But *ask* me, he would have said, and I would tell you that I had no recollections of passing through the town at all, so occupied was I with my musings. He was oblivious.

I want instead to cultivate more of what a friend calls an "attitude of gratitude." Like my friend Marge does. "When I get distracted or 'dry up' spiritually," she once told me, "I simply sit in my prayer spot—a chair in the corner of my living room. And if I'm having trouble, I look out the window and start with prayers of simple thanksgiving—for the diamonds of dew on the grass, for the translucent pink of a baby rabbit's ear backlit by the sun. I think, *This is all a gift*. Then I take it one step further, to think about my children, who are even greater gifts to be grateful for."

∽

I notice a paradox in my prayer, drawn from some unknown ancient century and said in prayer services by unnumbered members of Eastern Orthodox churches. *Grant that we so pass [the day's] hours in the perfect freedom of your service, that at eventide we may again give thanks to you, through Jesus Christ our Lord.* The "perfect freedom" of service? Service too often speaks to our culture of harsh servitude, cramping of style, the limiting of personal options.

But this prayer suggests that serving God is the way to freedom—the way not only to begin the day, but the way to end it, to pause at evening and *again give thanks to you*. In both movements—thanking God and serving God—the focus shifts. I find myself lifted out of myself. I discover the joy of not living as a self-centered, little-minded, sour-tasting captive to my whims and wants. No, I find freedom in living for Someone greater and far more worthy of gratitude than my own over-involved self.

In many ways, I know that focusing on serving God will mean I'll sometimes end the day more tired, perhaps more spent.

And yet, somehow, more full, more fulfilled. I think, *What if I lived in such yieldedness to God, lived in exuberant thanks for blessings that stud every step of where I walk, that I thought first of* him? *And thought last of God, at the end of the day?*

This is not Pollyanna denial, I tell myself. Paul the apostle, who was, after all, no stranger to hardship and persecution, told his followers, "Be joyful always; pray continually; give thanks in all circumstances" (1 Thessalonians 5:16–18). Even the hardest times, the busiest times, the dullest times contain traces of a goodness worthy of grateful thanks, all our waking hours.

Longing for Home

Lord, I am an inhabitant
Traveling from my country to yours.
Teach me the laws of your land,
Its way of life, its spirit,
So that I may truly find my home there.[110]

—WILLIAM OF ST. THIERRY

SOMETIMES I THINK PRAYER SHOULD MAKE me feel more at home in the world. More nestled snugly into the life I lead. More reconciled to the way things are. This morning, groggily waking up, I think of how I just want to *enjoy* this day.

But the prayer I use this week warns me not to grow too comfortable. True, "this is," as the children's hymn puts it, "my Father's world." I am a householder of this land, a citizen of my time. I need to live fully and gratefully where I have been put. But I also sojourn and have my eyes set elsewhere. For all my desire for settledness as I know it, I will never go far without longing for what is to come. For I also hold citizenship in God's country. I live for a way of life more like what I will know in heaven.

This way of life I taste in part, but in another sense I must wait for it. Because I hold citizenship in a world on the way, I want not to become a complacent fixture in the here and now. I am a tenant, or, as one book title aptly puts it, a "resident alien."

I will in some sense always know I am made for another existence. I live fully in the moment and yet aim past it.

This perspective, I realize this morning, never allows me to grow too entrenched, too settled. I should not be surprised at a welling up of Homesickness. A homesickness for a world I have yet to experience directly yet sense deeply in the here and now.

Richard Kew, a friend of mine, a man who grew up in England and now lives in the United States, knows what it is to realize a current home is not the only one. "Ours is a world full to overflowing with wanderers," he wrote. "Millions have left homes and all that is familiar to board trains, planes, or automobiles and make a new life for themselves across the country or the world. Some have been forced to flee their homeland, often on foot and in great peril, while others have moved because of work or opportunities. I have been a part of this huge human migration." So many of them are searching for a home. And he knows what that longing feels like. "For someone who lives far from the land of his or her birth," he says, "these sensations of 'exile' are themselves shadows of the greater exile of each of our souls from our eternal home."[111]

∞

One of my earliest memories from childhood concerned a longing for home. It provides a glimmer of what William of Thierry, a little-known monk and abbot writing more than eight hundred years ago, alluded to in his prayer.

I was nearing the end of my first day of kindergarten. It was time for Mom to pick me up, and she was nowhere in sight. I scanned the faces and the line of cars filling the curb outside my classroom. And I could not see her, at least not right away. I knew how much I wanted to get home, and, looking up and down the sidewalks intersecting the pavement in front of the school, I realized I did not know my way. Of course, I would not *have* to. She *would* come. But I panicked a little. How I wanted my familiar yard and room and perch in front of the living room TV!

Mom did come, of course, and all was well. We walked home together while I told her of my first day of school. But for an instant I knew deep longing for her and home.

Experiences like that help me understand why something about this prayer, when I found it in a collection of prayers from many lands, moved me. Its images of longing and wanting help to know the way resonated. They articulated a longing in my own heart.

William of St. Thierry, born of a twelfth-century noble family, surrounded by wealth and prestige, knew that his world, for all its comforts, held few truly rich satisfactions. He longed for a truer home, and in his quest he submitted to the life of poverty and simple living common for monks of the religious order he joined. His would not be an easy life, but he lived with radiant convictions about where his ultimate citizenship lay.

❧

It is another day. The metaphors not only move me, they have, as I have suggested already, unsettle me. Today I remember that part of living God's way means letting go of the familiar. And because life—at least life with God—has more to do with traveling on than sitting still, life will be full of moments of leaving behind the security of the solid and known. There is risk in any journey.

I recall the first leg of a cross-country flight I once took.

Normally I am perfectly at ease while flying, but this time I found myself compressed into a thirty-seat (or less) twin-engine commuter plane. As the craft accelerated down the runway for take-off, the wall panels quaked violently. The windows shook ominously. And all I could hear in the cabin was the swelling roar of engines laboring under the stress of lift-off. As the land fell suddenly away from us, I gripped my armrest—white-knuckled.

Many are the instances I have had to give up the security of solid ground. Leaving home for school. Beginning the adventure of marriage, then parenting. Heeding the call to give up one vocational path to follow another. My comfortable surroundings sometimes gave way to the necessary uncertainties of change. I have even felt suspended in midair, sensing a call to leave the familiar securities while not yet seeing a clearing where God is about to take me, like Abraham of old, of whom we read, "By faith Abraham, when called to go to a place he would later receive as his inheritance, obeyed and went, even though he did not know where he was going. By faith he made his home in the promised land like a stranger in a foreign country; he lived in tents, as did Isaac and Jacob, who were heirs with him of the same promise" (Hebrews 11:8–9). Such "precarity," as Dorothy Day, a kind of Mother Teresa for an earlier generation, put it, is far from a rarity in the life of obedience and faith.

The apostle Paul knew it. He could not recall his life's journey without including mention of unexpected turns: "Five times I received from the Jews the forty lashes minus one. Three times I was beaten with rods, once I was stoned, three times I was shipwrecked, I spent a night and a day in the open sea, I have been constantly on the move." I see few guarantees in a life that included being "in danger from rivers, in danger from bandits, in danger from my own countrymen, in danger from Gentiles; in danger in the city, in danger in the country, in danger at sea; and in danger from false brothers." Most of us would find it strange indeed to live a life about which we would say, "I have labored and toiled and have often gone without sleep; I have known hunger and thirst and have often gone without food; I have been cold and naked" (2 Corinthians 11:24–27). Yet that was the pattern of at least one person's life of faithfulness.

I have uncertainties, too—far less than Paul's, of course. I have trouble getting off my mind the job I have just interviewed for, directing an organization devoted to helping churches pray. I know I could do the job, and all indications are that I will be offered the position. But is it right? Much is in flux, too, with both my wife and me exploring ordination in the Episcopal Church. So many changes could be on the way!

So why do I think uncertainty should be a stranger to me as a Christian?

> *Lord, I am an inhabitant*
> *Traveling from my country to yours.*

And I should not always expect to feel perfectly comfortable. I experience what Peter Marshall, the Scottish Presbyterian who was chaplain to the Senate in the 1940s, called the "exile heart." While he led a rich life in the States, he said he often longed for the cottage in which he grew up, the smell of the damp Highland heather, a longing he knew ultimately partook of his longing for his ultimate home in God. A longing I experience today, in little ways. A longing that will not—should not—go away. For it keeps me moving toward my place, eternally in God.

ࢯ

This prayer helps me not only remember where my true home will be found, but it also encourages me to seek help for living in this place and time in light of that greater reality.

> *Teach me the laws of your land,*
> *Its way of life, its spirit,*
> *So that I may truly find my home there.*

This reminds me of how often Jesus spoke of the kingdom of God as something here but not yet "at hand," and yet to come in greater fullness. Already, Jesus was saying, we live in its reality. Already, the ways of peace and compassion, what Paul would come to call the law of the Spirit, inject their power into daily choices. We are to live as though the kingdom has arrived, even while we pray "your kingdom come."

And so we dream of a world as it could be; we work toward life for others as it can be. We long for Christ's mind and heart, for his ways to become our ways. I stand far from realizing the reality of that way of life, but I can always pray for it.

I am soon to lead a retreat focused on the spiritual life writer Henri Nouwen. As I prepare, I come across a passage that speaks powerfully to how I am praying and trying to live this week. Nouwen writes of how worry displaces us, leads us from our true home, our deepest center. It fragments our lives, he says: "The many things to do, to think about, to plan for, the many people to remember, to visit, or to talk with, the many causes to attack or defend, all these pull us apart and make us lose our center. Worrying causes us to be 'all over the place,' but seldom at home.

One way to express the spiritual crisis of our time is to say that most of us have an address but we cannot be found there. We know where we belong, but we keep being pulled away in many directions, as if we were still homeless."[112]

May I find another way, O God! I want to live with a view of my true home,

> *[i]ts way of life, its spirit,*
> *So that I may truly find my home there.*

The Ear of My Heart

Let me learn from you, Lord, you who are the truth. Put the ear of my heart next to your lips.[113]

—AUGUSTINE

WE CONSTANTLY, SOMEONE ONCE SAID, CARRY on an inner conversation, a kind of hidden dialogue, and we do it with one of three persons: our own self, another person, or God. Such internal dialoging helps us think and process what happens to us. But it also makes for a constant interior chatter. Rarely are the voices in our minds quieted.

This week's prayer of Augustine, like the prayer of his that moved me early in this year of praying with my mentors, tells me that I need to *listen*, not just carry on a monologue. I uncover a richer life by living and listening for truth outside of myself. I need to grow still enough to catch a larger, more compelling Voice. I need my heart's ear placed near God's lips.

In our times of "getting in touch with your feelings," that represents a profoundly different approach. Our culture stresses the primacy of knowing what we are sensing at any moment—and acting on it. I know I tend to live with my ear cocked for my own desires. We become experts on ourselves—instant and passionate authorities on our preferences in coffee, clothes, cars, neighbors. We know what we want and why we want it. And we want it now.

But I try, as this day begins, to start with another, gentler exercise in hearing. *Place the ear of my heart next to your lips.* Because I believe God does eloquently reveal truth in many ways—through circumstances, through Scripture, through a "still, small voice," even through intimate silence—I want to cultivate what a friend calls a state of "alert stillness."

The word *obedience,* say those who know Latin, comes from a root word that means "to listen." We found our lives on what is true and lasting when we manage at least for moments at a time to quiet the noisy, distracting voices within, and open ourselves to the true God. To obey requires a heart that cries out to be taught the truth, one that turns often to One who is not stingy with his wisdom and guidance.

∽

Such is the posture I need this week. I have another interview soon for the director's position of the prayer fellowship. How much I need guidance! So I ask God to help me hear. I don't want to miss the best that God intends in the choices I will have soon to make.

But this morning as I spend time with Augustine's prayer, I sense a deeper meaning. The issue is not pumping God for answers for a future just out of sight. God is no jukebox into which we put quarters and then wait for our selection to play. Mostly I live more deeply in God's truth by cultivating what someone calls a familiar friendship with Christ. I don't need answers as much as a relationship. I need to become more intimate with the One who holds the future.

Jesus likened the kinship between himself and his followers as that of a shepherd who knows his flock intimately, a flock that knows his signals and calls and prods. "[H]is sheep follow him because they know his voice. . . . I am the good shepherd; I know my sheep and my sheep know me—just as the Father knows me and I know the Father—and I lay down my life for the sheep. . . . I give them eternal life, and they shall never perish; no one can snatch them out of my hand (John 10:4, 14–15, 28).

Surely it is no accident that Augustine prays about the ears of his *heart*—the center of emotion and volition—and not just his mind. The movements of the heart, more than the synapses of the brain, are where I become convinced of truth. It is in the realm of my deep longings that I yield to God. The word I need in order to live comes through my subterranean self. And the biggest issue, I realize today, has to do with entrusting myself into the hands of God. And then not holding back.

〰

Augustine's simple, moving prayer appears in a section of his great masterpiece, *Confessions*. In book 4, where the prayer occurs, he tells of his years among the Manicheans, a strange religious group that Augustine would eventually repudiate as false and under the pall of great darkness. In this section he also tells of taking a mistress, becoming attracted to astrology, and to his great grief, losing a dear friend in death. Here is the summary of this time, a summary that introduces his prayer about learning to hear God's truth and listen for his voice:

> During this period of nine years from my nineteenth year to my twenty-eighth, I went astray and led others astray. I was deceived and deceived others, in varied lustful projects—sometimes publicly, by the teaching of what men style "the liberal arts"; sometimes secretly, under the false guise of reli-

gion. In the one, I was proud of myself; in the other, superstitious; in all, vain! In my public life I was striving after the emptiness of popular fame, going so far as to seek theatrical applause, entering poetic contests, striving for the straw garlands and the vanity of theatricals and intemperate desires. In my private life I was seeking to be purged from these corruptions of ours by [the practice of the false Manichean religion]. These projects I followed out and practiced with my friends, who were both deceived with me and by me. . . . But now, O Lord, these things are past and time has healed my wound.[114]

After the false starts of his young adulthood, how well Augustine learned to seek God! He gladly received the clean truth God showed him. And so Augustine continued to pray, *Let me learn from you, Lord. . . . Put the ear of my heart next to your lips.*

I see now that the point of this day, this week, this year, is not so much that I get every choice "right," every vocational cue down pat, not that I perfectly manage my schedule and become a model parent. I may not always have pristine certainty about every door I must open or close. But I can live in the assurance that God will tell me what I truly need to know. God will guide me with his eye upon me (Psalm 32:8). Most important for me is that I cultivate a heart that steadfastly seeks what is true by opening all of my life to the God of truth.

Teach me your truth, O God, wherever it leads.

So I will pray today and this week, believing the effort won't be in vain. That God will indeed tell me what I must know to be faithful.

CHAPTER FIFTY

A God Named Sovereign

*O Sovereign LORD, you have begun to show to your servant
your greatness and your strong hand. For what god is there in
heaven or on earth that can do the deeds and mighty works
you do? Let me go over and see the good land beyond the
Jordan—that fine hill country and Lebanon.*[115]

—MOSES, THE PROPHET

AT FIRST I DIDN'T REALIZE THAT I HAD
stumbled onto such a poignant prayer—one filled with as
much mingled longing and trust as any in the Bible. The great
Old Testament leader Moses speaks in these verses, as his lifetime
of sojourning nears its end. *You have begun,* the hoary prophet
prays with vast understatement, *to show to your servant your greatness and your strong hand.*

I chose this passage because, with my needing to make a crucial decision, I wanted to saturate my week with awareness of God's
power and goodness. I needed a refresher course in God's attributes.
So I turned to my concordance and looked up the word *greatness.*
Here in Deuteronomy was one of the first instances it appeared.
Moses names God as sovereign and calls God strong. The passage
rings with triumph. That seemed straightforward enough.

Little did I know, as I say, how much pathos lay behind it. For
the God who showered on Moses and the people lavish mercy he

comes also as a God who will not wink at rank faithlessness. Moses, destined by God to lead his people Israel to the promised land, has just learned of some unsettling consequences. There has been a change in plans. He will not live to possess the land. He cries out to God for reprieve.

Why this disturbing turn? The people, earlier verses reveal, "set out from Horeb and went toward the hill country of the Amorites . . . which the LORD our God is giving" (Deuteronomy 1:19–20). But then they became, Moses reminds them, "unwilling to go up; you rebelled against the command of the LORD your God. You grumbled in your tents and said, 'The LORD hates us; so he brought us out of Egypt to deliver us into the hands of the Amorites to destroy us'" (Deuteronomy 1:26–27).

With all the signs and wonders along the way, the Israelites' grumbling could only mean they had turned their backs on God. They chose instead to nurse the sickly sweet sin of hopelessness. "Despair is the absolute extreme of self-love," suggests Thomas Merton. "It is reached when a [person] deliberately turns his [or her] back on all help from anyone else in order to taste the rotten luxury of knowing himself [or herself] to be lost."[116] Such was Israel's state when the people groaned and resisted God.

And so the Lord, sovereign and inscrutable just as he is intimate and loving, swears that not one of that "evil generation" will see the good land, none except faithful Caleb. Which means *not Moses.* We can guess that Moses felt deflated, even devastated. It does not seem fair!

And so comes Moses' plea: *Let me go over and see the good land beyond the Jordan.*

God will not leave him without consolation. But God does not answer Moses' cry directly. God will not give all Moses wants, when he wants it. Moses' dream will be deferred again.

How much of life entails waiting, I reflect. Moses knew this through all his life, to say nothing of this juncture. I know it at this juncture of mine.

The decision weighing on me this week grows out of my interviews for the position with the Anglican prayer organization. The search committee just offered the job. So much about the role seems to fit with my interests and aspirations. But something doesn't seem right.

Jill, when we prayed about it with some trusted friends, had trouble shaking the impression that the prospect was a "decoy": that while on the surface it seemed to fit, ultimately it fell short of God's best plan for me. And in the interviews I glimpsed how administrative the position would be, how consumed with the daily details of an organization I would be compelled to become. How would such work fit my still-vibrant calling to ordination? It would not seem to answer my growing call to pastor. Still, the committee that interviewed has their hopes set on me. I feel great pressure to accept. Even some entrusted with my ordination process seem intent on my moving forward with the position.

Nevertheless as I pray I believe I hear, *Don't go forward. Wait.* This may represent a concrete, financially stable opportunity. Not a bad career move, should I look at it that way. But that does not make it right.

And so I turn to God and affirm again, *what god is there in heaven or on earth that can do the deeds and mighty works you do?* I call to mind again how good God is. How his guidance can be trusted. Why do anything but wait in trust?

"I discovered," writes Sue Monk Kidd, "that in the spiritual life, the long way round is the saving way." Sometimes trusting what someone called the "slow work of God" vividly emerges as our best option.

But isn't waiting, a voice inside Sue seemed to whisper, really just procrastination—"a nice idea, maybe, but something misplaced in the fast-paced, demanding world of today"? Besides, she reasoned, "I didn't *want* to wait. Waiting seemed the rawest kind of agony. I wanted God to simply whisk away the masks I had spent most of my life fashioning, . . . to solve my problems, heal my wounds, and alleviate the inexplicable sense of discontent and pain I was feeling. And mind you, I wanted all of this *now,* immediately, or at the very least soon.

I was a typical quickaholic."[117]

So am I. I do not live well in the uncertainty that waiting entails. And so Moses becomes my inspiration. Moses, who makes my petty delays seem minor indeed. Moses, who even amid his crushed hopes still blessed God.

Last night I said to Jill, "Sometimes I wish I had a 'normal' vocation. I don't fit easily into traditional categories. I seem driven to live by a sense of call, sometimes in some unusual configurations. Sometimes I pay the cost of that." Often I feel impatient to know how things will unfold.

But how faithless my frustration! Why ask for what is easy when what I most want is what is right? For often enough, I get glimpses of other possibilities that keep me going, that leave me grateful and excited. Truer glimpses that resonate deeply with who I sense God has made me to be. And so I walk on. I put one foot in front of another.

Today I called the chair of the Anglican search committee. I could hear the disappointment in his voice. But I knew how I had to answer.

The call over, I tell myself, *There is something else ahead, something better. No need to jump ahead of God.* Oh, the flooding relief that comes now that all is settled! For the moment.

⟲

After Moses' pleading, finally God said, "Do not speak to me anymore about this matter. Go up to the top of [Mount] Pisgah and look west and north and south and east. Look at the land with your own eyes, since you are not going to cross this Jordan" (Deuteronomy 3:26–27).

What did Moses see in the faraway vista? Certainly enough to know God's promises to his people were indeed being fulfilled. Enough to keep him walking. Enough to keep him praying with hope.

I Am Safe

Answer me when I call to you,
  O my righteous God.
Give me relief from my distress;
  be merciful to me and hear my prayer. . . .
Know that the LORD Has set apart the godly for himself;
  the LORD will hear when I call to him. . . .
You have filled my heart with greater joy
  than when their grain and new wine abound.
I will lie down and sleep in peace,
  for you alone, O LORD,
  make me dwell in safety.

—DAVID, THE PSALMIST

ANXIETIES, SUCH AS I EXPERIENCE TODAY, sometimes trouble my sleep. They do not keep me from drifting off at night; *that* never seems a problem when I drop into bed tired. No, they awaken me well before the alarm, stabbing me awake and making it hard to fall asleep again.

As they have this morning.

Some of my worries have to do with my eight-year-old. Bekah, bright and vivacious, is nevertheless continuing to have a hard time in school, not meshing well with her teacher. Yesterday I had literally to pry her out of the car as we pulled up curbside for the start of the school day; she cried and wanted nothing less than to go in.

And other little worries nag at me. My deadlines. Jill's back pain and fatigue. And I have yet one more interview with the denominational commission on ministry to discuss my desire to be ordained.

But this week's prayer from Psalm 4 tells me that even while we sleep (or lie waiting for sleep), wonderful things move forward. God does not forget to sustain a universe alive with activity. Why lie awake scheming and worrying about what will and won't get done?

∾

I saw a TV documentary on night shifts, on the hidden legions of workers who punch in on their time clocks at the time most of us set our alarm clocks at retiring. The documentary followed a night watchman, an emergency room nurse, a mail order warehouse worker, an Internet web page operator. What a world of commerce and production and communication goes on while most people sleep! People deliver our groceries, hold their feverish children, and sort our mail. A vast network hums along while we, submerged in sleep, do nothing more than dream or turn over.

But that is just a parable, in a way, for other larger, unseen forces that keep watch, pull weight, oversee, and superintend.

In *The Book of Common Prayer* I sometimes read a blessedly simple prayer from the late-night service for Compline:

Keep watch, dear Lord, with those who work, or watch, or weep this night, and give your angels charge over those who sleep. Tend the sick, Lord Christ; give rest to the weary, bless the dying, soothe the suffering, pity the afflicted, shield the joyous; and all for your love's sake. Amen.[118]

How much does God do in my slumbering absence!

> *Indeed, he who watches over Israel*
> *will neither slumber nor sleep* (Psalm 121:4).

∽

Yesterday, out running along my town's roads I saw at one brick two-story ranch a red cardinal arcing up from a shrub just under a large front window. The bird flew smack into the pane of glass, its swift flight halted with a clatter of beak and claw. It dropped downward, only to fly at the window, flay at the glass yet again. I had seen a bird do that at the same window, last week. *What is it about that glass?* I wondered. *Why do birds keep crashing into it?*

I paused in front of the house, peering inside. I could barely make out what I saw, but there it was, the explanation: an indoor hanging flowering plant, suspended from the ceiling behind the window. The glass formed an invisible barrier even while it offered a constant view, a nonstop attraction for the cardinal's frustrated efforts.

Sometimes I approach my tasks and callings with similarly frenetic, futile efforts. I get agitated. I forget life does not all hinge on my flitting and pushing and pulling. There is a better way.

> *You have filled my heart with greater joy*
> *than when their grain and new wine abound.*
> *I will lie down and sleep in peace,*
> *for you alone, O LORD,*
> *make me dwell in safety.*

Why not depend more fully on God? I ask myself. *You have filled my heart with greater joy,* I tell God. *Why should I fear?*

This morning I remember who keeps constant watch when I rise, just as God did while I slept. Yes, there is much on my desk waiting for my attention. Decisions to make. Children and a wife who rightfully expect my attention. But something is different today. I notice how late in the morning it is already . . . and how sound my sleep has been.

Perfect Hope

Christ be with me
Christ be in me,
Christ before me,
Christ behind me,
Christ beside me,
Christ to win me
Christ to comfort
And restore me.

—CELTIC BLESSING

THIS PRAYER PENNED BY AN ANONYMOUS writer (though it is often mistakenly attributed to St. Patrick) found its way to me from a friend who wrote, in part, to tell me of a wonderful experience. The prayer appeared on the front of the card, a Celtic-flavored blessing an artistic friend of hers had designed and colored.

Inside the card my friend had written about reading a book on prayer, as she lay helpless on her bed from acute pain from a slipped disk. She had no way to contact her husband, away at work. She closed her eyes and felt a nudge to ask God for healing light.

When she opened her eyes she found the room streaming with a beam. Was it coincidence? She was not instantaneously healed, but, she wrote, "The good news is that I made a faster recovery than during my last episode."

She felt she had been visited. Even more significant than her swifter-than-normal recovery was how immediate God seemed to her, a God who draws close and comes alongside.

∞

My prayer for this week, filled seemingly with every kind of preposition of relationship, accepts Christ's presence as a given and yet at the same time asks for it as though it were not. God is present. Always. And yet I invoke and invite with a yearning heart. And the prayer reminds me that nothing matters more than who accompanies me through this day, this life. I never move into the unknown future without the presence of One who goes

> *with me . . .*
> *in me . . .*
> *before me . . .*
> *behind me . . .*
> *beside me.*

All sides are covered!

∞

Just concluded: a final interview meeting with the committee overseeing ordination in my diocese. I'm still not sure what they will decide, but I know I have been obedient. I know only good will come of the process.

And I know again, as I finger the card printed with my prayer for this week, that Someone ushers me into today and tomorrow. Moves forward with me and guides. That allows me to end my year of praying with spiritual mentors on a more certain note than I began. Yes, there is that uncertain road ahead, as I prayed in my first prayer of Thomas Merton's: *I do not see the road ahead of me, I cannot know for certain where it will end.* But I am hopeful. Not because of any outcome I may or may not predict accurately, but because I can hope in the constancy of a God who promises never to leave me or forsake me. Christ in me, to echo Paul's phrase in Colossians 1:27, also goes along *with* me. Before me and behind me. I can always go forward. I can always trust.

"Perfect hope," writes Thomas Merton, "is achieved on the brink of despair when, instead of falling over the edge, we find ourselves walking on the air. Hope is always just about to turn into despair, but never does so, for at the moment of supreme crisis God's power is suddenly made perfect in our infirmity."[119]

∽

Jill prayed out loud for me this morning. She asked God to fill me with assurance that God goes behind me and before me. She didn't know I was praying this prayer from centuries ago, how her own words echoed my own. She could not know at the time how on the mark such a request is for me. How crucial, I suspect, it is for all of us.

Acknowledgments and Permissions

7. "Antiphon to God the Father" by Hildegard of Bingen, from *Hildegard of Bingen,* ed. by fiona Bowie and Oliver Davies, copyright 1990, published by Crossroad Publishing Company. Used by permission.

8. "The Source of Everlasting Blessing," from *Celtic Christian Spirituality,* ed. by Oliver Davies and Fiona Bowie. Copyright Oliver Davies and Fiona Bowie, 1995. Reprinted by permission of the Continuum Publishing Company, New York.

9. Prayer by Saint Ephraim the Syrian taken from *A Spiritual Psalter* (verses of spiritual poetry by Saint Ephraim the Syrian, collected and translated by Bishop Theophan the Recluse), translated by Antonina Janda, copyright 1997 The St. John Kronstadt Press, 1180 Orthodox Way, Liberty, TN 37095; www.kronstadt.org.

10. Episcopal blessing on page 191 from *The Book of Occasional Services* 1994, © 1995 Church Pension Fund.

11. *A Guide to Prayer for Ministers and Other Servants* by Rueben P. Job and Norman Shawchuck. Copyright 1983 The Upper Room. Used by permission.

Notes

1   Eugene H. Peterson, *Answering God* (San Francisco: Harper & Row, 1989), 19.

2   Anthony Bloom, *Courage to Pray* (Crestwood, N.Y.: St. Vladimir's Seminary Press), 37–38.

3   Frederick Buechner, *Now and Then* (San Francisco: Harper San Francisco, 1983), 2–3.

4   Thomas Merton, *Thoughts in Solitude* (New York: Farrar, Straus and Giroux, 1956, 1958), 79.

5   Henri Nouwen, *With Open Hands* (Notre Dame, Ind.: Ave Maria, 1972), 57.

6   C. S. Lewis, *Letters to Malcolm, Chiefly on Prayer* (San Diego, Calif.: Harcourt Brace Jovanovich, 1963, 1964), 82.

7   C. S. Lewis, *Surprised by Joy* (New York: Harcourt, Brace & World, 1955), 228–229.

8   Toyohiko Kagawa, *Meditations on the Cross* (Chicago: Willett, Clark, 1935), 112.

9   Kenneth L. Wilson, *Have Faith without Fear* (New York: Harper & Row, 1970), 54.

10 Saint Augustine, *Confessions* (*X.xxvii [38]*) (Oxford, Engl.: Oxford Univesity Press, 1991), 201.

11 Henri J. M. Nouwen, *Making All Things New* (San Francisco: Harper & Row, 1981), 67.

12 John Donne, *Selections from* Divine Poems, *Sermons,* Devotions, *And Prayers,* ed. John Booty (New York: Paulist, 1990), 299.

[13] "Preface of Lent," *The Book of Common Prayer* (New York: The Church Hymnal Corporation, 1979), 219.

[14] Eugene Peterson, *Subversive Spirituality* (Grand Rapids, Mich.: Eerdmans, 1994, 1997), 30.

[15] Philip Yancey, *What's So Amazing About Grace?* (Grand Rapids, Mich.: Zondervan, 1997), 181.

[16] Eugene Peterson, *The Contemplative Pastor* (Carol Stream, Ill.: Christianity Today, Inc./Word, 1997), 110.

[17] Patrick, "St. Patrick's Hymn Before Tara," trans. James Mangan, in *Poetry for the Soul* (Nashville: Moorings, 1995), 222.

[18] Patrick, *Confession,* II:16, author's adaptation.

[19] Patrick, "St. Patrick's Hymn Before Tara."

[20] The Rev. S. Baring-Gould, *The Lives of the Saints, vol. 3* (Edinburgh: John Grant, 1914), 296–297.

[21] *Ibid.,* 298.

[22] Patrick, "St. Patrick's Hymn Before Tara."

[23] *Confession,* II:12, author's adaptation.

[24] Chirstina Rossetti, "Who Shall Deliver Me?" in *Poetry for the Soul,* 420.

[25] John W. Crawford, "Christina Rossetti," Frank N. Magill, ed., *Critical Survey of Poetry, vol. 6* (Pasadena, Calif.: Salem, 1992), 2809.

[26] Thomas Merton, *Entering the Silence* (San Francisco: Harper San Francisco, 1996), 5.

[27] Source unknown.

[28] Adapted by the author from several sources.

[29] Issac Singer quoted in *Answering God,* 36–37.

[30] Dick Eastman, *Celebration of Praise* (Grand Rapids, Mich.: Baker, 1984), 34.

[31] *Ibid.*

[32] Ronald Rolheiser, *The Shattered Lantern* (New York: Crossroad, 1995), 66.

[33] Source unknown.

[34] A. Gilchrist, ed, *Life and Works of William Blake,* quoted in Mary Oliver, *West Wind* (Boston: Houghton Mifflin, 1997), 1.

[35] Christopher de Vinck, *Simple Wonders* (Grand Rapids, Mich.: Zondervan, 1995), 61.

[36] Ellis Peters, *A Rare Benedictine* (New York: Mysterious Books/Warner, 1979, 1981, 1988), 110–11.

[37] Betty Shannon Cloyd, *Children and Prayer* (Nashville: Upper Room Books, 1997), 27–28.

[38] John A. Cutter, "Move Over Midlife Crisis," *The Tennessean,* June 7, 1998.

[39] Ludovicus (Juan Luis) Vives quoted in George Appleton, ed., *The Oxford Book of Prayer* (Oxford, Eng.: Oxford University Press, 1985), 117–118 (author's adaptation).

[40] Saint Thérèse of Lisieux, *The Autobiography of Saint Thérèse of Lisieux,* trans. John Beevers (New York: Image/Doubleday, 1957), 26.

[41] Benedict J. Groeschel, *Spiritual Passages* (New York: Crossroad, 1983), 4–5.

[42] William H. Shannon, *Anselm: The Joy of Faith* (New York: Crossroad, 1999), 31–32.

[43] Sophy Burnham, *A Book of Angels* (New York: Ballantine, 1990), xii.

[44] Duane W. H. Arnold, comp., *Prayers of the Martyrs* (Grand Rapids, Mich.: Zondervan, 1991), 26.

[45] "I want to know Christ and the power of his resurrection and the fellowship of sharing in his sufferings, becoming like him in his death" (Philippians 3:10).

[46] Soren Kierkegaard, *Purity of Heart Is to Will One Thing* (New York: Harper & Brothers, 1938), 98.

[47] Anonymous, *The Martyrdom of Ignatius* in *Ante-Nicene Fathers, volume 1.*

[48] A version of this story appears in Helen Waddell, The Desert Fathers (London: Constable, 1936, 1987), 157–158.

[49] Gregg Easterbrook, "What Came Before Creation?" *US News & World Report,* July 20, 1998, 46.

[50] Some of this material appeared in my book *21 Days to a Better Quiet Time with God* (Grand Rapids, Mich.: Zondervan, 1998), 119–120.

[51] Soren Kierkegaard, *Purity of Heart Is to Will One Thing* (New York: Harper & Brothers, 1938.

[52] Teresa of Avila, *The Interior Castle* (Sixth Mansions, chap. 1), E. Allison Peers, ed. and trans., online edition (http://www.ccep.org).

[53] *The Imitation of Christ,* Book 3, chapter 3.

[54] Introduction to a translation in progress, *The Imitation of Christ* by Thomas à Kempis, translated by Henry William Griffin, to be published by Harper San Francisco. Used with the permission of the author.

[55] *Ibid.*

[56] Julian of Norwich, *Encounter with God's Love,* Upper Room Spiritual Classics, vol. 2, ed. Keith Beasley-Topliffe (Nashville: Upper Room Books, 1998), 17.

[57] Ronald Rolheiser, *The Shattered Lantern* (New York: Crossroad, 1995).

[58] Julian of Norwich, 16.

[59] Original source unknown.

[60] Andrew Murray quoted in Maxie Duham, *The Workbook of Common Prayer* (Nashville: The Upper Room, 1979), 40.

[61] Thomas Merton, *Thoughts in Solitude* (New York: Farrar, Straus and Giroux, 1956, 1958), 104.

[62] Friedrich von Hügel, *Letters to a Niece,* quoted in *The Spiritual Formation Bible* (Grand Rapids, Mich.: Zondervan, 1999), 975.

[63] Eadmer, *Vita Anselmi,* quoted in William H. Shannon, *Anselm: The Joy of Faith* (New York: Crossroad, 1999), 31.

[64] Madame Guyon, *The Autobiography of Madame Guyon,* chapter 5.

[65] *Ibid.*

[66] Haddon Robinson, quoted in Paul D. Robbins, "The Back Page," *Leadership,* Summer 1987.

[67] Hildegard, ed. Fiona Bowie and Oliver Davies, trans. Robert Carver, *Hildegard of Bingen* (New York: Crossroad, 1990), 112.

[68] Women in the Medieval Church," *Christian History,* Issue 30, 1997.

[69] Jane Kenyon, *Notes from the Other Side,* quoted in "Reflections," *Christianity Today,* July 10, 2000, 45.

[70] Timothy Jones, *Awake My Soul: Practical Spirituality for Busy People* (New York: Doubleday, 1999), xi.

[71] Source unknown.

[72] C. S. Lewis, *Reflections on the Psalms* (New York: Harcourt, Brace, 1958), 91–92.

[73] The title (and whereabouts) of the book in which I found this little prayer now escapes me.

[74] Thomas Merton, *New Seeds of Contemplation* (New York: New Directions, 1961), 180.

[75] Rebecca J. Weston, "A Breakfast Prayer," *Table Graces for the Family* (Nashville: Thomas Nelson, 1964).

[76] Grace M. Jantzen, *Julian of Norwich* (New York: Paulist, 1988), 156.

[77] *Ibid.*

[78] *Ibid.,* 215.

[79] Simone Weil, *Waiting for God* (New York: Harper & Bros., 1951), 112.

[80] Esther de Waal, *The Celtic Way of Prayer* (New York: Doubleday, 1997), 210–11.

[81] Eugene Peterson, *Answering God,* 87.

[82] Esther de Waal, *The Celtic Way of Prayer* (New York: Doubleday, 1997), 210.

[83] *Ibid.,* 211.

[84] Larry Woiwode, "A Fifty-Year Walk," *Books and Culture,* November/December 1998, 12.

[85] Thomas Merton, *Praying the Psalms,* quoted in Esther de Waal, 210.

[86] Eugene Peterson, *Answering God,* 35.

[87] Timothy Jones, *The Art of Prayer* (New York: Ballantine, 1997), 175–176.

[88] Ephraim of Syria, excerpted and adapted from a prayer in Mary

Batchelor, ed. *The Doubleday Prayer Collection* (New York: Doubleday, 1992, 1996), 318.

89 "Prayers and Thanksgivings," *The Book of Common Prayer,* 814.

90 Avery Brooke, *Finding God in the World* (New York: Harper & Row, 1989), 1.

91 Eugene Peterson, *Answering God,* 71.

92 Frederick Buechner, quoted in *Listening to Your Life* (San Francisco: Harper San Francisco, 1992), 2.

93 Thomas Merton, *Thoughts in Solitude,* 3.

94 *The Book of Occasional Services* (New York: Church Hymnal Corporation, 1984), 23.

95 Quoted in David Adam, ed., *The Wisdom of the Celts* (Grand Rapids, Mich.: William B. Eerdmans, 1996), 18.

96 M. Craig Barnes, *Yearning* (Downers Grove, Ill.: InterVarsity Press, 1991), 16.

97 Lewis Smedes, *Standing on the Promises* (Nashville, Thomas Nelson, 1998), 15.

98 St. Ephraim the Syrian, *A Spiritual Psalter* (verses of spiritual poetry by St. Ephraim the Syrian, collected and translated by Bishop Theophan the Reduse), trans. Antonina Janda (Liberty, Tenn.: The St. John of Kronstadt Press, 1990), 76.

99 *Ibid.,* 240.

100 TR, *Revelations,* Book 2, author's rendering.

101 *Ibid.*

102 Jean-Pierre de Caussade, *Abadonment to Divine Providence,* trans. John Beevers (New York: Image/Doubleday, 1975), 36.

103 Thomas à Kempis, *The Imitation of Christ,* Harold C. Gardiner, ed. (New York: Image/ Doubleday, 1955), 117.

104 Soren Kierkegaard, *Purity of Heart Is to Will One Thing.*

105 Gerrit Scott Dawson, *Heartfelt* (Nashville: Upper Room Books, 1993), 56–57.

106 Rueben Job and Norman Shawchuck, *A Guide to Prayer for Ministers and Other Servants* (Nashville: Upper Room Books, 1983), 46.

107 Henri J. M. Nouwen, *The Living Reminder* (New York: Seabury, 1977), 11.

108 Quoted in *The Doubleday Prayer Collection*, 280.

109 Kathleen Norris, *The Cloister Walk* (New York: Riverhead, 1996), 1.

110 William of St. Thierry, adapted from a prayer in *Doubleday Prayer Collection*, 148.

111 From a book in process. Used by permission of the author.

112 Henri J. M. Nouwen, *Making All Things New* (San Francisco: Harper & Row, 1981), 36.

113 Augustine, *Confessions,* Book 4, Chapter 5, author's rendering.

114 *Confessions, ibid.*

115 Deuternonomy 3:24–25.

116 Thomas Merton, *New Seeds of Contemplation* (New York: New Directions), 180.

117 Sue Monk Kidd, *When the Heart Waits* (San Francisco: Harper San Francisco, 1990), 20–21.

118 *The Book of Common Prayer,* 134.

119 Thomas Merton, *No Man Is an Island* (New York: Harcourt Brace Jovanovich, 1955), 206.